Bears' Guide to the Best MBAs by Distance Learning

John Bear, Ph.D.
Mariah Bear, M.A.

Additional writing and research by
Clinton Marsh

Ten Speed Press
Berkeley   Toronto

Other Degree.net Books:
Bears' Guide to Earning Degrees by Distance Learning
College Degrees by Mail and Internet
Bears' Guide to the Best Computer Degrees by Distance Learning

Degree.net
A division of Ten Speed Press
PO Box 7123
Berkeley, California 94707
www.degree.net

Distributed in Australia by Simon & Schuster, in Canada by Ten Speed Press Canada, in New Zealand by Southern Publishers Group, in South Africa by Real Books, in Southeast Asia by Berkeley Books, and in the United Kingdom by Airlift Books.

Cover design by Cale Burr
Text design by Jeff Brandenburg, ImageComp

Library of Congress Cataloging-in-Publication Data on file with publisher.

First printing this edition, 2000
Printed in Canada

1 2 3 4 5 6 7 8 9 10 -- 05 04 03 02 01 00

Dedications

John's:
For Nikoli and Tristan, MBA candidates for the class of 2021.

Mariah's:
For Joe, the best darn husband ever.

Acknowledgments

We would like to thank all of the school employees who made the job of putting this book together so much easier, by promptly and pleasantly responding to queries, making sure the information was up to date, and so on. In addition, we would like to thank Clinton Marsh for the substantial writing and research support that he brought to the project, Leslie Bolick for cheerful performance of even the most thankless tasks, Karen Stein for the proofreading, Jeff Brandenburg for speedy, accurate, and sparkly typesetting and design, and Cale Burr for yet another in a series of fabulous covers.

Contents

Suffolk University http.//www.suffolk.edu

Appendices

1. Introduction to Distance Learning: A 150-Year-Old Idea Whose Time Has Come

Distance learning has never been hotter. With the advent of the Internet, compressed video, courses on software, interactive CD-ROM, and other great new technologies, the idea of earning a degree from the comfort of your own home seems utterly modern. But, in fact, distance learning has a long and distinguished history. In the early years of the 19th Century, as the British empire was sending its politicians, its bureaucrats, and its merchants to the far corners of the world, the need arose for these people, now living in such remote places as Hong Kong, Johannesburg, and Chicago, to earn good British university degrees. The University of London was established to solve this problem, and it was based on quite a radical idea for the time: the notion that you could earn credit, certificates, and eventually degrees based on what you know, regardless of how you learned it. Then and now, many of the degrees of the University of London are earned entirely by passing examinations.

In other words, if you know enough about business or psychology or accounting or marketing to pass an examination, you'll get the credit, and the degree, whether you gained your knowledge by sitting in classrooms for years, by studying on your own, or by apprenticing yourself to an expert.

This approach to education and certification arrived in America in time to benefit the likes of young Abraham Lincoln, who couldn't afford to "go away" to law school, but instead studied on his own, by firelight, until he had learned enough to pass the Illinois state bar exam. The state of Illinois, thankfully, didn't care where he got his knowledge, as long as he could demonstrate it by passing their exam.

Distance learning grew slowly and steadily for decades, and then really took off in the 1970s, when entirely new nonresident universities were established, and some major state schools (like the University of Iowa and the University of Oklahoma) established distance learning units within their schools. It is now truly possible to earn a Bachelor's or a Master's degree in almost any field of study without ever leaving home, except perhaps to take a local examination. This is a boon to working adults who want or need a degree for advancement, but just can't take the time off work, and professional degrees, such as MBAs, have become a real growth area for distance learning.

One reason is that it is increasingly true that a degree, particularly one in a specialized, competitive business field, can be more useful than experience alone. You may be the best business manager, accountant, or strategist in three counties, but all too often, if you don't have a piece of paper certifying you as a Master of Business Administration, you may miss out on the better jobs and higher salaries that go to MBA-holders, regardless of their competence.

But how useful are these degrees by distance learning? As long as they are earned from legitimate, properly accredited schools, they are at least as useful as the "old-fashioned" degrees earned by sitting in classrooms and lecture halls for years. Indeed, in one major study conducted by the National Institute of Education, many personnel and HR people said they *preferred* the degrees earned at a distance, in part because their employees took less time off work, and in part because such degrees demonstrate an admirable level of ability to work on one's own, without constant supervision. And now that Internet and other types of technology-based learning are an integrated part of many companies' training programs, distance degrees are practically mainstream. Graduates who, twenty years ago, might have balked at saying, "I got my degree by correspondence," are proud to say, "I earned my degree on the Internet." Same coursework, different world.

That phrase mentioned above, "properly accredited," is key, since there are not only a distressing number of fake schools (degree mills) around (as there have been for 600 years!), but also quite a few "gray area" schools that claim to be accredited, but, in fact, are accredited by agencies they started themselves, which are not recognized by the U.S. Department of Education or by the CHEA, the Council on Higher Education Accreditation in Washington.

Chapters 4 and 5 discuss accreditation in greater depth and tell you how to check out a school. With the ease of Internet advertising, it has become all too common for sleazy schools to put up a great web site and make all sorts of claims. Many of the good schools, on the other hand, rarely advertise or promote themselves, either because they don't know how to do so effectively, or because they think it unseemly. And most of the bad schools—the illegal or barely legal diploma mills—advertise all the time, in major national newspapers and magazines. This book will help you separate fact from fiction.

Many readers will choose to deal only with the schools listed in this book. These listings may not represent *every* good distance MBA program. Schools keep developing programs, and it is inevitable that more good ones will go on-line as this book goes to the printer.

In the next chapter, we'll discuss MBAs and other related degrees, and introduce you to this book's various helpful sections.

2. MBAs and Distance Learning: What's in This Book

The Master of Business Administration is one of the most popular and sought-after degrees available today. As the world moves to an increasingly corporate and service-based economy, companies have an ever-growing need for business savvy and certain sets of technical skills. And an MBA-holder is likely to have those skills and savvy. Indeed, according to a recent *New York Times* article, "the term MBA has become synonymous with raw business talent. Pay scales have risen accordingly, and overall, the future looks bright for MBA students."

In 1965, fewer than 10,000 MBAs were granted to U.S. students. In 1977, the number rose to 48,000, and in 1998 it was 94,000. Even more interesting, some two-thirds of these degrees are awarded not to full-time students, but to part-time or distance students, often subsidized by their employers. These are people looking to move up at their jobs, move to more rewarding careers, or even start their own businesses. According to a survey conducted by the Graduate Management Admission Council, about 20 percent of the people who get MBAs are planning to go into business for themselves.

Many are older, and about 30 percent of graduates have families. In distance-learning programs, that percentage jumps even higher, because a distance-learning MBA allows students to study at their own pace, without interrupting work or family life.

Degree Options

In this book, we have chosen to list not just MBAs, but also other useful graduate programs in the general area of business. The reason for this is simple: There is no industry standard for what is taught in an MBA, and, as an example, for some readers, an MS (Master of Science) in finance may be just as useful—or more so—than an MBA with a finance concentration. Indeed, "business administration" is such a broad term that it can encompass degrees focusing on airport administration, tourism and hospitality, healthcare, or legal studies, as well as more traditional areas, such as accounting, economics, and human resources. A procedural note: For simplicity's sake, we'll refer the "MBA programs" in the chapters to come, to mean all programs in this book. (For instance, "A few MBA programs offer some credit for life-experience learning.") In the individual school listings, however, we make it very clear which degree will be awarded.

Our criteria for including a school are as follows:

1. It offers an MBA, or a Master's degree in a practical, business-related field.

2. The school is accredited, according to GAAP (Generally Accepted Accreditation Principles), or a current candidate for regional accreditation. For a full explanation of this, see chapter 5.

3. The degree can be earned either fully at a distance, with no visits to the school, or with relatively short residential sessions. Residency requirements are clearly spelled out in each school's listing.

As we noted in the introduction to this book, these listings represent the best schools that meet these criteria *to the best of our knowledge, at presstime.* Distance learning is such a hot and growing field that good programs may very well debut the week this book hits the shelves. Mildly annoying, of course, but it's the way of the world.

If a program looks good and isn't listed in this book, we recommend that you check it out using the hints given in chapters 3 and 4. And please, let us know about any exciting new programs you come across. If we've heard about them, and there's a reason they're not in the book (i.e., the school is a clever phony, or we've heard other bad things about it) we'll e-mail back and let you know (or write to you by mail, if you enclose a self-addressed, stamped envelope). If it's a new program, we'll write it up in the next edition, and we'll be sure to thank you on the acknowledgments page to boot. You can e-mail the authors at:

john.bear@degree.net or mariah.bear@degree.net

or write to us at

John and Mariah Bear
Degree.net
C/O Ten Speed Press
PO Box 7123
Berkeley, CA 94707 USA

What's in This Book

Here's a quick point-by-point on the chapters that follow, why we included them, and what to expect.

Chapter 3: Choosing the Right MBA for You. Before you start investigating programs, you should know what you're looking for. Sounds easy, right? Here's a list of eleven factors you may not have considered that will help you pick a program that's not just good, but that's right for *you*.

Chapter 4: Checking Out a School. We've said it before, we'll say it again: Deal with one of the schools in this book, and you won't be ripped off. But as there are so many other schools out there—some great, some quite non-wonderful—you need to know how to evaluate them. This chapter and the one following give you the tools you need.

Chapter 5: Accreditation. Perhaps the most important question you can ask is whether a school is accredited. Not all unaccredited schools are bad, and not all accredited schools are fabulous but, in general, you're safest dealing with a school that has GAAP accreditation. We'll tell you how to know for sure. A special section discusses professional accreditation for business schools. Those that have it say it's vital; those that don't (and that's the majority) disagree. We clear it up for you.

Chapter 6: Applying to a Business School. How many schools should you apply to? Must you have a Bachelor's degree? Do you have to take the GMAT? Should you invest in an MBA counseling service to help you apply? These and other questions answered.

Chapter 7: Alternative Ways of Earning Credit. Most MBA programs have fairly rigid courses of study, but many do allow transfer credit, and some accept life-experience credits as well. This chapter briefly discusses these options.

Chapter 8: Distance-Learning Technologies Defined. What the heck is compressed video, anyway? How do on-line classes differ from discussion groups? Do I absolutely have to have a computer to take a distance learning course? Basics of distance-learning technology explained in easy-to-understand language.

Chapter 9: Schools Offering the MBA by Distance Learning. The core of this book, this chapter profiles 100 institutions offering distance graduate degrees in business fields, complete with full contact information, web sites, prerequisites, entrance requirements, and any special features we think you should know about.

Appendix A: Schools Offering Regional Distance MBAs. Some schools offer distance learning, but only to students within their state, or local area. The reasons may be lack of funds or faculty, technological limitations, or simply that they aren't set up to deal with students from around the globe. This chapter lists 23 such schools, sorted by region. If you live in the region served, such a school may well be a good option, as you can have closer contact with faculty and fellow students.

Appendix B: Schools Offering a Bachelor's in Business Administration. In the interest of providing a wide range of options for distance scholars interested in business fields, we offer this list of 55 accredited institutions offering an undergraduate business administration degree.

Appendix C: Schools Offering Correspondence Courses. This list includes forty-eight accredited schools offering distance courses in graduate business fields. You can use these courses to meet prerequisites, get transfer credit, or maybe just get in-depth knowledge of a field without taking the plunge and enrolling in a full degree program.

Appendix D: For More Information on Schools in This Book. Basic contact information.

Appendix E: For More Information on Schools Not in This Book. Research hints.

Appendix F: For Personal Advice on Your Own Situation. A consulting service started by co-author Dr. John Bear.

Appendix G: Bending the Rules. Hints and tricks for making the most of just about any situation.

Index of Concentrations and Specializations: Looking for that MBA in international tourism? Wondering about making the most of your human resources background? This handy at-a-glance index shows which schools offer which concentrations for their advanced degrees.

3. Choosing the Right MBA for You: Eleven Vital Factors

As we've already discussed, there's a world of MBA (and other useful business-related) programs out there. Which one is right for you? There are absolutely no right or wrong answers here. Each person is different, and each person's needs, both present and predictable future ones, are different. The following list gives eleven things you may wish to consider in deciding which programs to pursue. After each item, we've summarized the decision you need to make on that item. Remember, the more thought you put into this now, the better match that MBA program will be for you.

Slant 1: Specialized vs. General

There are a number of courses that appear, in one form or another, in just about every MBA program on earth: finance, economics, marketing, strategic planning, and so on. But beyond those, there are literally hundreds of different subjects that have been included in MBA programs, either as stand-alone courses, or as part of a specialized MBA program, where just about every course has a certain slant: not just marketing, but marketing for the automotive industry; not just organizational behavior, but OB for the military; not just accounting, but accounting for the medical profession.

Many people are not only content with a generic, or "plain vanilla" MBA, they prefer to have a degree without any specialization. They argue that if they were to change careers, their degree would stand them in good stead regardless of their new chosen field. Others feel that a specialized MBA—say, in healthcare administration, or church management, or banking, or international trade and finance—will be a better ticket of entree to jobs in those professions.

YOU NEED TO DECIDE: Will a specialized MBA best suit your career needs, or will you be better off with a more general business education?

Slant 2: Theoretical vs. Practical (or More Math vs. Less Math)

How important is it to understand technical theories that may drive the commodities market up or down? What do we know about the causes and aftermath of major economic recessions in the seventeenth and eighteenth centuries? Can sophisticated economic modeling help a high-tech company's long-term strategic planning? Is it more important to learn how to write a business plan in short order, or to spend a year understanding the underlying nature of business plans and the ways in which corporate behaviors are shaped by them?

These differing approaches are one of the main reasons that some MBA programs require a good deal of high-level mathematics, including advanced calculus, while others are content to offer nothing beyond elementary algebra and beginning statistics.

Note: Many of the more practical programs (and some of the others) require internships, in which students work for real-world companies.

YOU NEED TO DECIDE: Do you want a theoretical or a practical education? (Of course, many programs provide both, but there is usually a slant one way or the other.) If you just want to get the information and apply it quickly to your career, practical may be the way to go. If you're looking to be a "big picture person," maybe even to teach or to advance to a doctoral level, theoretical may be your best option. Weigh the balance of these two approaches and decide if the school has what you need.

Cost: Lower Cost vs. Higher Cost

There is not a whole lot of correlation between the cost of an education and its quality. In our part of the country, for instance, there are two wonderful schools, Stanford and Berkeley. The former costs about five times as much as the latter, but even the most diehard Cardinal fan would not argue that the Stanford education is five times better.

The total cost of an MBA can range from the vicinity of US$5,000 to well over $100,000 (when you take into account tuition, fees, housing, travel, and, most significantly for the non-distance-learners, time lost from your job). Many students can get funding, in the form of employer subsidies, student loans, or grants. But it is important not to fall into the trap of thinking that an MBA that costs under $10,000 must have something wrong with it. Research the program, see if it offers what you need, and then decide if you can afford it.

YOU NEED TO DECIDE: What you can afford to pay. You need to remember that more expensive is not always better, and to research your funding options.

Worldview: National vs. International

Some schools are in business to train people to work in the country where the school is located, or at least in that region of the world. Others pay special attention to the growing globalization of the economy, and the increasing numbers of business people who may work in two or three or more countries in the course of their career.

These differences are often reflected in the kinds of courses offered, and the approach taken in the courses. As one simple example, there are certain basic accounting principles that are the same anywhere in the world. And yet there are some significant differences in generally accepted accounting principles as they are practiced in the U.S. versus in Japan, or Russia, or Saudi Arabia. If a student is considering an MBA in order to be a better manager of a lumberyard in Michigan, then it may not matter to him or her that human resource practices are dramatically different in China than they are in the U.S. But if that person gets involved in buying or selling products in Asia, or needs to understand NAFTA, or needs to remit or deposit foreign currencies, then he or she could benefit from an international approach.

YOU NEED TO DECIDE: Whether an international focus is important to you and, if so, you need to be sure the program you choose meets that need.

Reputation: Big vs. Modest

There are a small number of schools that are world-famous, either as entire universities (for instance, Harvard, Stanford, Oxford), or especially as MBA-granting business schools (for instance Henley, Wharton, and Chicago).

These schools, and others like them, regularly appear on the "ten best" or "25 best" or "world's best" lists published annually by magazines such as *Business Week*, *U.S. News and World Report, Canadian Business,* and *The Economist.* These "best" lists vary slightly from year to year—programs change and, probably more importantly, magazines need to tell at least a somewhat new story each year. But the great majority of good, decent, usable MBA programs, surely more than 90 percent of those with recognized accreditation, never make any lists at all.

Undeniably, some people choose a school because of its reputation. They believe it will help them in the job-finding or internal promotion process, and they may be right. They believe that a person who finishes near the bottom of his or her graduating class at Harvard or Yale will get ahead faster than the person who finishes first in his or her class at some obscure little school in Nebraska, Montana, or the English Midlands. They, too, may be right in certain circumstances. If you were a recruiter for your company, which would you choose? There is no simple answer to this question. It is simply a factor to keep in mind during the school selection process. Most of the schools in this book aren't in that top-prestige echelon. (On one magazine's list of "top 25" MBA programs, only two were available by distance learning.) Why? A number of reasons. One, older schools may be a bit more conservative, less likely to try out new approaches and new technologies. Also, these ultra exclusive schools may feel that they have all the students they need, and thus have no impetus to expand their offerings. We predict that this will change as distance learning becomes more and more mainstream, especially as it is not only accepted but welcomed in so many top corporations today.

YOU NEED TO DECIDE: Is prestige vitally important to you? If so, be prepared to pay more and meet more stringent entrance requirements.

Interactiveness: Low vs. High

There are distance MBA programs in which the degree can be earned literally without ever talking to another human being: read the textbooks, take the exams, and earn the degree. There are others in which the hallmark of the program is its interactivity. Each student is expected to be either on-line or on the phone or at meetings of local cohort groups for quite a few hours each week. And there is a wide range of models in between.

Similarly, there are people who prefer working on their own, perhaps with the option of being able to ask a question of a faculty member if the need arises. And there are others who thrive on the group process, sharing ideas, gaining insights from others, and regularly getting a sense of how well they are doing.

The simple advice here is that if this matter is important, then it is wise to choose a program with a model that matches your preferred style.

YOU NEED TO DECIDE: How much supervision do you want or need, how much interaction with students and professors, and so forth. Do you want to set your own pace or have regularly scheduled on-line courses? The school listings in chapter 9 make it clear what level of interaction each program requires.

Exams: Many, Few, or None

Some people would rather suffer medieval torture than take a major do-or-die exam. Some, on the other hand, thrive on the challenge of exams. And many are willing to tolerate them, but quite often would rather be somewhere else, thank you.

Since there are distance MBA programs with a variety of academic models, it is often wise to choose one that matches your preferences with regard to exams. European Bachelor's degree programs are often based largely or entirely on examinations, and that is also the case with many European MBAs, where the only requirement is passing a series of course exams. American Master's programs are often graded based on demonstrations of ability, including writing term papers, interaction with faculty and other students, quizzes, and exams. Since some schools put a lot less weight on exams than others, this could be a factor when you are shopping around for the ideal program.

YOU NEED TO DECIDE: How you feel about exams, and how much other work you're up for if you choose a program lighter on the exams and heavier on other assignments.

Thesis or Major Paper: Yes or No

Master's programs of all kinds traditionally require a major paper, called a thesis in America and a dissertation in Britain, as a means of demonstrating that you have a certain level of mastery of the field. But there are programs that offer a choice, such as ten courses plus a thesis or thirteen courses without a thesis. Some allow some sort of other major project, such as implementing and testing systems at the workplace. And there are those that do not offer a thesis option at all. Some students feel that a thesis is not only a good opportunity to do significant work in one's field but also the thesis itself can make a good addition to one's CV or portfolio of career experiences. Others, especially those with less experience doing a single major project, may feel that a wider array of course work is just as satisfactory.

YOU NEED TO DECIDE: Whether or not you want to do a thesis or final project.

Degree Title: MBA vs. MA or MS or Others

As we've discussed in prior chapters, not all schools award the MBA degree, while others offer both MBAs and other Master's degrees in business subjects, such as an MA or MS in business administration, or business studies, or just business. This might be just fine, or it might even be better than an MBA for your purposes, depending on what your career goals are and how you plan to use your degree.

YOU NEED TO DECIDE: Exactly what degree title you want—or, at least, whether an equally useful degree with a different name would suit your purposes. The listings in chapter 9 make it clear what degree(s) each school awards.

Time Involved: 8 or 9 Months to 3 or More Years

Most academic degree programs have a pretty standardized length. A Bachelor's degree in the U.S. will require about 120 semester hours, which typically will take four years to earn. A Bachelor's in the U.K. will require three years or a bit more. An American Master's degree in most fields is from 30 to 36 semester units in length.

The MBA alone seems extremely variable in this regard. While European MBAs often take one year (which can mean anything from 8 to 12 months), there are others that are designed to require 18 to 24 months. And while many American MBAs take two academic years (16 to 20 months), there are some that require a year and a half, and some as little as one year. Many distance programs offer part-time options, allowing you to stretch the course of study out so as not to conflict with work and family—or, conversely, to do many courses at once, so as to finish more quickly.

YOU NEED TO DECIDE: How long you'd like the program to take. Whatever you decide, within reason, you can probably find a program to suit your needs.

Going on for a Doctorate: Yes, No, or Maybe

Many, but by no means all, doctoral programs require that the student have earned a Master's degree first. There are a moderate percentage of such schools, perhaps one-fourth to one-third, that do not consider an MBA degree as meeting their Master's degree requirement for entry into a doctoral program. They argue that the MBA is a professional degree, not an academic one, and that the main reason for earning a Doctorate is to enter the academic world.

Accordingly, this minority of schools says that people planning eventually to earn a Doctorate should do an MA or an MS in finance or marketing or economics or other business field, but not the more general MBA. But the remaining two-thirds to three-fourths of doctoral programs *do* consider an MBA as meeting their Master's requirement. Accordingly, if going on to a particular doctoral program is a possibility, it would be appropriate to learn the policy of that doctoral school in this regard.

YOU NEED TO DECIDE: Whether you plan to go on for a doctorate. If so, you need to be sure that the degree you get will suit your needs. If you have any questions, ask an admissions counselor whether holders of that degree have gone on to doctoral studies, and at what schools. If you know the school at which you intend to get that doctorate, ask them whether the MBA is acceptable.

4. Checking Out a School

Two Problems, Two Questions to Ask

An MBA program is, for many people, one of the most expensive and time-consuming things they will do in their lives. And yet some people will spend more time and energy choosing a refrigerator or a television set than they will selecting a school. For such people, one of two major problems may set in later:

Problem One: There Are Unpleasant Surprises Down the Road

Some people enroll in good, legitimate schools, but then discover that the program just doesn't suit their needs. For instance, while most MBAs have an analytical or mathematical bent, others are most focused on people management or leadership. There's also the possibility that an MBA isn't exactly what you want—perhaps an MS in management would serve the same purpose as well or better (despite its title, this book does include a number of non-MBA programs that may suit readers' needs). Or maybe the school's sales reps said the program could be finished in two years, but a closer reading of the catalog shows that only a full-time, nonworking student could accomplish this.

Thus there are two kinds of "checking out" to do: Will the school meet my needs? And, is the school legitimate?

Question One: Will It Meet My Needs?

You'd think people would learn this before spending thousands of dollars and years of their lives. But we have received hundreds of letters from people who had very unpleasant surprises after enrolling, or even after graduating. It is essential that you satisfy yourself that a given school will meet your needs before you spend any money. Make sure you know exactly what it will cost (no hidden "graduation fees," for instance), whether your employer will accept (and perhaps pay for) your degree, whether any relevant licensing agencies will accept the work, and so on.

Problem Two: The School Turns Out to Be Less than Wonderful

Some people enroll in a school that seems to suit their needs without looking at it very closely. And then, when they see their alma mater exposed on *60 Minutes* or *20/20*, they wail, "But I didn't know; they had such a lovely catalog." Now clearly, if you apply to one of the schools listed in this book, that won't be a problem. All of these schools have proper accreditation, whether regional, DETC, or national (see chapter 5 for an explanation of these terms). Still, it's our experience that some people will buy a book such as this, note all of the accredited schools, and still end up studying at a less-than-wonderful institution. Why? Well, maybe it was less expensive, or seemed easier to do, and it swore that it was just as good as the schools in this book.

In addition, there's the fact that good, accredited programs will almost certainly debut after this book does (distance learning being such an active, growing field). So, you may well be faced with advertisements or web sites for interesting-looking MBA programs that aren't listed here, and you need to know how to evaluate them. Are they new, fabulous programs that came on-line after our researchers finished their work, or sleazy diploma mills waiting to rip you off?

Question Two: Is It a Good School?

If you have any doubts, concerns, worries, or hunches about any school, whether in this book or not, you have every right to check it out. It's a buyer's market.

You can ask any questions you want about accreditation, number of students, credentials of the people in charge, campus facilities (some schools with very impressive-looking catalogs are operated from mail-forwarding services), and so on. Of course, the school has the right not to answer, whereupon you have the right not to enroll. For ways and means of getting more information, see appendices D and E.

For specifics on accreditation, including how to tell if a school is properly accredited, read the next chapter.

5. Accreditation: Why It's So Important

Many books and articles about choosing the right school say that the most important thing is to choose an accredited school. Unfortunately, some of these authors stop there, without making clear that there are many different kinds of accreditation, at least one of which is not only useless, but often worse than having no accreditation at all. Indeed, many less-than-wonderful schools (you won't find them in this book) start their own accrediting agencies, which are often just another button on their telephones, so that they can advertise that they are indeed accredited.

Regional Accreditation

In the United States, there are six regional accrediting agencies, each with jurisdiction for one region of the country: Western, Northwestern, Southern, New England, Middle States, and North Central. These accreditors deal with entire colleges or universities, not just with the schools of business or the MBA programs. So when, for instance, the North Central Association says that Bellevue University in Nebraska is accredited, that means that all of the schools, colleges, and departments within that university have regional accreditation. To find out whether a school has regional accreditation, you can contact the accreditors, or go to their web site to check the school out. They can be reached as follows:

Middle States Association of Colleges and Schools
Commission on Higher Education
3624 Market Street
Philadelphia, PA 19104
(215) 662-5606 • Fax: (215) 662-5950
E-mail: info@msache.org
Web site: www.msache.org
Delaware, District of Columbia, Maryland, New Jersey, New York, Pennsylvania, Puerto Rico, Virgin Islands

New England Association of Schools and Colleges
209 Burlington Road
Bedford, MA 01730-1433
(617) 271-0022 • Fax: (617) 271-0950
E-mail: info@neasc.org
Web site: www.neasc.org
Connecticut, Maine, Massachusetts, New Hampshire, Rhode Island, Vermont

North Central Association of Colleges and Schools
30 North La Salle Street, Suite 2400
Chicago, IL 60602
(800) 621-7440 • Fax: (312) 263-7462
E-mail: info@ncacihe.org
Web site: www.ncacihe.org
Arizona, Arkansas, Colorado, Illinois, Indiana, Iowa, Kansas, Michigan, Minnesota, Missouri, Nebraska, New Mexico, North Dakota, Ohio, Oklahoma, South Dakota, West Virginia, Wisconsin, Wyoming

Northwest Association of Schools and Colleges
11300 NE 33rd Place, Suite 120
Bellevue, WA 98004
(206) 827-2005 • Fax: (206) 827-3395
E-mail: selman@uwashington.edu
Web site: www.idbsu.edu/nasc
Alaska, Idaho, Montana, Nevada, Oregon, Utah, Washington

Southern Association of Colleges and Schools
1866 Southern Lane
Decatur, GA 30033
(800) 248-7701 • Fax: (404) 679-4558
E-mail: jrogers@sacscoc.org
Web site: www.sacs.org
Alabama, Florida, Georgia, Kentucky, Louisiana, Mississippi, North Carolina, South Carolina, Tennessee, Texas, Virginia

Western Association of Schools and Colleges
Box 9990, Mills College
Oakland, CA 94613-0990
(510) 632-5000 • Fax: (510) 632-8361
E-mail: wascsr@wasc.mills.edu
Web site: wasc.mills.edu
California, Hawaii, Guam, Trust Territory of the Pacific

National Accreditation

The Distance Education and Training Council is a recognized national accrediting agency dealing with schools that offer most or all of their training through distance learning. Like the regional accreditors, they only accredit entire colleges or universities, not departments within universities. There are a dozen or so DETC-accredited schools that offer MBA programs, typically 100 percent by distance learning. While the DETC accreditation process is a rigorous and responsible one, it remains the case that DETC accreditation does not have as wide an acceptance as regional accreditation. Not all regionally accredited schools will accept DETC-accredited degrees, and there are job descriptions and corporate reimbursement plans that require a regionally accredited degree.

Distance Education and Training Council
1601 18th Street NW
Washington, DC 20009
(202) 234-5100 • Fax: (202) 332-1386
E-mail: detc@detc.org
Web site: www.detc.org

Professional Accreditation

In addition to regional accreditation, there are more than seventy professional accrediting associations that deal with specific departments or schools within a college or university. For instance, the American Psychology Association deals only with departments of psychology. In the field of business, there are three different accrediting associations that accredit not entire universities, but just the colleges or schools of business. Anyone can start his or her own accrediting agency, but to be useful, these professional accreditors need to be recognized either by CHEA, the Council on Higher Education Accreditation (an independent non-governmental agency in Washington) or by the U.S. Department of Education, or both.

The **International Association for Management Education**, formerly the American Assembly of Collegiate Schools of Business (and, confusingly, still referred to as the AACSB) is the oldest business school accreditor and is widely regarded as the most prestigious, dealing with the business schools at Harvard, Yale, Stanford, Chicago, Northwestern, and dozens of others.

The **Association of Collegiate Business Schools and Programs** offers professional accreditation to already-regionally-accredited schools of business at smaller colleges and universities.

The **Accrediting Council for Independent Colleges and Schools** deals primarily with business colleges, community colleges, and vocational schools, but it also accredits a small number of MBA-granting business schools.

How important is professional accreditation? Schools accredited by AACSB often suggest this accreditation puts them a cut or two above the rest, and there are some corporate hiring officers who would agree. On the other hand, there are hundreds of well-regarded MBA programs in regionally-accredited universities that do not have professional accreditation, many of whose graduates would attest to the value of their education and the usefulness of their degree. This matter is just one factor of many in choosing a school.

Contact these professional accreditors at:

The International Association for Management Education
600 Emerson Road, Suite 300
St. Louis, MO 63141-6762
(314) 872-8481 · Fax: (314) 872-8495
Web site: www.aacsb.edu

The Association of Collegiate Business Schools and Programs
7007 College Boulevard, Suite 420
Overland Park, KS 66211
(913) 339-9356 · Fax: (913) 339-6226

The Accrediting Council for Independent Colleges and Schools
750 First Street NE, Suite 980
Washington, DC 20002-4241
(202) 336-6780 · Fax: (202) 482-2593
E-mail: acics@acics.org
Web site: www.acics.org

Non-U.S. Accreditation

Different words are used to describe the process of accreditation or school validation in different countries, such as the Royal Charter in Great Britain. In many countries, this process is rigorous, and requires a careful investigation of the school and its programs. But in some countries, most of them very small, something called "accreditation" is granted almost automatically, even to schools that don't even have a campus in that country.

International Accreditation

Many of the less-than-wonderful schools claim to be "internationally accredited," typically by an agency with the words "International" or "World" or "Global" in the title. In the world of higher education, there is no recognized or accepted or useful concept of international accreditation. These so-called international accreditors may operate legally in their country, but it is safe to say that no university registrars, government agencies, and few if any corporate human resources professionals would accept their accreditation. There are, needless to say, no schools with "international" accreditation in this book.

No Accreditation at All

No new school is properly accredited when it opens for business. It typically takes several years of operation before one can apply to a recognized accrediting agency, and then the process may take anywhere from one to six years. So if a school states that it is not accredited, this is not necessarily a bad thing. It may be too new. Unfortunately, some bad schools explain to potential students that they are not accredited because they are too innovative, or too unusual for the recognized accreditors, or that because they are international in scope, they do not need to be regionally or nationally accredited. One should take such claims with a grain of salt.

The Bottom Line: GAAP, the Generally Accepted Accreditation Principles

Things are really not nearly as complicated as they may appear from the above text, simply because there are plenty of distance-learning MBA programs that meet the international standards of GAAP, or Generally Accepted Accreditation Principles (the acronym is, of course, borrowed from the world of accounting). These principles, which are acceptable to virtually every university registrar, corporate human resources department, and government agency, require that a school meet any one of the following six criteria:

1. Accredited by an accrediting agency recognized by the U.S. Department of Education.

2. Accredited by an accrediting agency recognized by the Council on Higher Education Accreditation in Washington, D.C.

3. Listed in the *International Handbook of Universities* (a UNESCO publication).

4. Listed in the *Commonwealth Universities Yearbook*.

5. Listed in the World Education Series, published by PIER (Projects in International Education Research), a joint venture of the American Association of Collegiate Registrars and Admissions Officers and NBAFSA, the Association of International Educators, with the participation of the College Board.

6. Listed in the Countries Series, published by NOOSR, the National Office for Overseas Skills Recognition, in Australia.

If an MBA program does not meet any of these six criteria, that does not necessarily mean it is bad or fake. But it does mean that the degree will not be regarded as accredited, and may well prove troublesome to the holder. With so many distance-learning MBAs that do meet the criteria of GAAP, why take a chance?

6. Applying to Business Schools

How Many Schools Should You Apply To?

There is no single answer to this question that is right for everyone. Each person will have to determine his or her own best answer. The decision should be based on the following four factors:

1. Likelihood of admission

Some schools are extremely competitive or popular and admit fewer than 10 percent of qualified applicants. Some have an "open admission" policy and admit literally everyone who applies. Most are somewhere in between.

If your goal is to be admitted to one of the highly competitive schools (such as Duke or Purdue), where your chances of being accepted are not high, then it is wise to apply to at least four or five schools that would be among your top choices and to at least one "safety valve," an easier one, in case all else fails.

If you are interested in one of the good, but not world-famous, nonresident programs, your chances for acceptance are probably better than nine in ten, so you might decide to apply to only one or, preferably, two, just in case.

2. Cost

There is a tremendous range of possible costs for the MBA and similar degrees. The least expensive program in this book costs under $9,000, the most expensive over $82,000. As we discussed in chapter 3, this is a case in which "you get what you pay for" really doesn't apply. The prestige of a top-name school may open a few more doors, but there's no stigma attached to a good degree from an accredited school, even if it's not the most expensive and/or most famous (not surprisingly, the two factors often go hand in hand).

3. What they offer you

Shopping around for a school is a little like shopping for a new car. Many schools either have perpetual money needs or operate as profit-making businesses. In either case, they are most eager to enroll new students. Thus it is not unreasonable to ask the schools what they can do for you. Let them know that you are a knowledgeable "shopper" and that you have read this book. Do they have courses or faculty advisors in your specific field? If not, will they get them for you? How much credit will they give for your existing credentials? How long will it take to earn the degree? Are there any scholarships or tuition reduction plans available? Does tuition have to be paid all at once, or can it be spread out over time? If factors like these are important to you, then it could pay to shop around for the best deal.

You might consider investigating at least two or three schools that appear somewhat similar because there will surely be differences.

Caution: Remember that academic quality and reputation are probably the most important factors—so don't let a small financial saving be a reason to switch from a good school to a less-than-good school. Again, all the schools in this book are good, reputable institutions, but there are many shady operators out there who are eager to offer you a deal, take your money, and then award you a worthless or even dangerous degree. That may sound alarmist, but we talk to people every day whose careers or academic studies have been damaged by a bad degree.

4. Your own time

Applying to a school can be a time-consuming process—and it costs money, too. Many schools have application fees ranging from $25 to $100. Some people get so carried away with the process of applying to school after school that they never get around to earning their degree!

Of course, once you have prepared a good and detailed resume, curriculum vitae, or life-experience portfolio, you can use it to apply to more than one school.

Another time factor is how much of a hurry you are in. If you apply to several schools at once, the chances are good that at least one will admit you, and you can begin work promptly. If you apply to only one, and it turns you down, or you experience long delays, then it can take a month or two—or more—to go through the admission process again elsewhere.

Speeding Up the Admission Process

The admission process at most traditional schools is very slow; most people apply nearly a year in advance and do not learn whether their application has been accepted for four to six months. The schools in this book vary immensely in their policies in this regard. Some will grant conditional acceptance within a few weeks after receiving the application. ("Conditional" means that they must later verify the prior learning experiences you claim.) Others take just as long as traditional programs.

The following three factors can result in a much faster admission process:

1. Selecting schools by admission policy

A school's admission policy should be stated in its catalog. Since you will find a range among schools of a few weeks to six months for a decision, the simple solution is to ask and then apply to schools with a fast procedure.

2. Asking for speedy decisions

Some schools have formal procedures whereby you can request an early decision on your acceptance. Others do the same thing informally for those who ask. In effect, this puts you at the top of the pile in the admission office, so you will have the decision in perhaps half the usual time. Other schools use what they call a "rolling admissions" procedure, which means, in effect, that each application is considered soon after it is received instead of being held several months and considered with a large batch of others.

3. Applying pressure

As previously indicated, many schools are eager to have new students. If you make it clear to a school that you are in a hurry and may consider going elsewhere if you don't hear from them promptly, they will usually speed up the process. It is not unreasonable to specify a timeframe. If, for instance, you are mailing in your application on September 1, you might enclose a note saying that you would like to have their decision mailed or phoned to you by October 1. (Some schools routinely telephone their acceptances, others do so if asked, some will only do so by collect call, and others will not, no matter what.)

How to Apply to a School

The basic procedure is essentially the same at all schools, traditional or nontraditional:

1. You write, telephone, or email for the school's catalog, prospectus, or other literature, and admission form.

2. You complete the admission form and return it to the school with the application fee, if any.

3. You complete any other requirements the school may have (exams, transcripts, letters of recommendation, etc.).

4. The school notifies you of its decision.

It is step three that can vary tremendously from school to school. At some schools, all that is required is the admission application. Others will require various entrance examinations to test your aptitude or knowledge level, transcripts, three or more letters of reference, a statement of financial condition, and possibly a personal interview, either on the campus or with a local representative in your area.

Luckily, the majority of schools in this book have relatively simple entrance requirements. All schools should tell you exactly what they expect you to do in order to apply. If it is not clear, ask. If the school does not supply prompt, helpful answers, then you probably don't want to deal with them anyway. Remember, it's a buyer's market.

It is advisable, in general, not to send a whole bunch of stuff to a school the very first time you write to them. A short note asking for their catalog should suffice. You may wish to indicate your field and degree goal ("I am interested in the executive MBA program through distance learning") in case they have different sets of literature for different programs. It probably can do no harm to mention that you are a reader of this book; it might get you slightly more prompt or more personal responses. (On the other hand, we have gotten more than a few grouchy letters from readers who say, "I told them I was a personal friend of yours, and it still took six months for an answer." Oh, dear. Well, if they hadn't said that, it might have been even longer. Or perhaps shorter. Who knows?)

The Matter of Entrance Examinations

Many nonresident MBA programs do not require any entrance examinations, even at schools that do require exams for on-campus study. The main reason for this appears to be that nonresidential students do not contribute to overcrowding on the campus, so more of them can be admitted. A second reason is that nonresidential business students tend to be more mature, and often have real-world business experience, which means that the schools acknowledge they have the ability to decide which program is best for them, and the savvy to do well.

There are, needless to say, exceptions. If you have particular feelings about examinations—positive or negative—you will be able to find schools that meet your requirements. Do not hesitate to ask any school about their exam requirements if it is not clear from the catalog.

Graduate Admission Examinations

Again, many nonresidential schools do not require any entrance examinations (for business schools, this generally means the GMAT, although a few require the GRE, or allow applicants to take either). Sometimes, there's a two-tiered system: businesspeople with a certain amount of management-level experience (usually three to five years) do not need to take the GMAT, on the assumption that they already have the necessary business savvy. Those without the experience still need to take the test.

The GMAT, or Graduate Management Admission Test, has both verbal and math sections, and two essays. This test is no longer administered in the old-fashioned pen-and-paper mode, but electronically at testing centers. The advantage of this is that you can often get your results immediately (not including the essay marks, but these are less vital to your success), without waiting and worrying while they are mailed to you. The disadvantage is that now all questions must be answered in order, which means no skipping the tough ones and coming back to them later. You're also now penalized more severely for not finishing all of the sections. If you have questions about the test, the website is quite helpful, allowing you to purchase review books and software, as well as download sample essay topics for free.

Graduate Management Admission Test
Educational Testing Service
P.O. Box 6103
Princeton, NJ 08541-6103
(609) 771-7330
E-mail: gmat@ets.org
Web site: www.gmat.org

The GRE, or Graduate Record Examination, is also administered by the Educational Testing Service. The basic GRE consists of a $3^1/_2$-hour aptitude test (verbal, quantitative, and analytical abilities). While most business schools require the GMAT, a few do ask for the GRE instead, or accept it as a substitute. The GRE also offers subject exams, which test undergraduate-level knowledge. It is unlikely that you would be asked to take one of these for a business degree, although there are subject exams in economics, math, and computer science.

Graduate Record Examinations
Education Testing Service
P.O. Box 6000
Princeton, NJ 08541-6000
(609) 771-7670
E-mail: gre-info@ets.org
Web site: www.gre.org

English-Language Examinations

The Test of English as a Foreign Language, or TOEFL, is often required for applicants whose first language is not English. (We have listed several schools that offer non-English programs, simply because they serve large populations, or offer programs that would otherwise be of interest to many people. In general, however, the vast majority of the schools listed present their programs in the English language.) The TOEFL tests one's ability to read and write English at the level of college instruction. Some schools specify a required score for those who have English as a second or other language, others just say "sufficient TOEFL score required." Usually, this means in the range of 500 to 600 points. Schools with "live" instructors (on CD-ROM, over television, etc.) may also require the TOEFL test that evaluates comprehension of spoken English. The test is given at testing sites in close to 200 countries, 12 times a year.

Test of English as a Foreign Language
P.O. Box 6151
Princeton, NJ 08541-6151
(609) 771-7760
E-mail: toefl@ets.org
Web site: www.toefl.org

Exam Preparation

There are many excellent books available at most libraries and larger bookstores on how to prepare for the GMAT or GRE, complete with sample questions and answers. Also, the testing agencies themselves sell literature on their tests as well as copies of previous years' examinations.

The testing agencies used to deny vigorously that either cramming or coaching could affect one's scores. In the face of overwhelming evidence to the contrary, they no longer make those claims. Some coaching services have documented score increases of 25 to 30 percent. Check the Yellow Pages or the bulletin boards on high school or college campuses. You may well be able to find a local college or university extension program that provides good prep courses for a fraction of the fees charged by professional course providers. Expect to pay anywhere from $300 for a local college course to $1,000 for a professional course. The two main test preparation services are Kaplan and Princeton Review. Both also sell preparation books and software. To find out more about their services, go to www.kaplan.com or www.review.com.

Admissions Consultants

Some students seek help from professional MBA admissions consultants, to write a cutting-edge entrance essay, learn tips for getting into the best programs, or otherwise get a foot in the door. These services can be quite expensive (from hundreds to thousands of dollars, depending on the service used), and are probably not necessary for distance-education students. If you desperately want to get into a top-notch program, and fear that you won't be able to present yourself to the best effect, and especially if you're investigating residential programs as well as distance options, such a consultant may give you an advantage. Only about 1 percent of students at residential programs have used such services, and probably even fewer distance enrollees. Still, if you're worried about your chances, and you are willing to spend a fair amount of money, here are some resources:

Kaplan offers a service whereby applicants are matched up with former admissions committee members from the student's school of choice. For more information, call (800) KAPTEST, or go to www.kaplan.com/consulting.

A firm called MBA Strategies will do on-phone evaluations of candidates, and help in the editing of entrance essays. (619) 922-5991, www.mbastrategies.com

Accepted.com does phone consulting and offers on-line essay editing. (310) 392-1734, www.accepted.com

Finally, a company called Ivy Essays sells previously-accepted admissions essays for use as inspiration. (888) IVY-ESSA, www.ivyessays.com

Again, we stress that most distance students will never need these services, but for those who like to cover all of their bases and have the time and money to spend, these services have been successfully used by students at America's top schools.

7. Alternative Ways of Earning Credit

Most MBA programs have fairly rigid courses of study, but many do allow you to bring in some transfer credit, and some accept life-experience and/or exam credits as well. Each school listing tells what sort of credit the school allows, provided, of course, they gave us this information when we asked for it. Otherwise, if you have potentially applicable prior credits, or relevant life-experience learning, it never hurts to ask. Several schools, for instance, will waive courses if you have professional credentials. So, while your CPA certification may not technically grant you credits, it will allow you to skip one or more accounting courses. That sort of thing. Here are some other ways you may be able to earn credits: exams, life experience, foreign academic experience, and correspondence courses.

Equivalency Exams

Not many of the schools in this book accept equivalency exam credits, but a few do, and the exams they are most likely to accept are CLEP and PEP. These are exams that, once you take them, give you credits equivalent to having taken a college course. Usually, this is taken as equivalent to an undergraduate course, but there are graduate programs that will allow the credits as well.

CLEP (the College-Level Examination Program) and PEP (the Proficiency Examination Program) administer equivalency exams at hundreds of testing centers all over North America, and, by special arrangement, many of them can be administered almost anywhere in the world.

CLEP is offered by the College Entrance Examination Board, known as "the College Board" (Rosedale Road, Princeton, NJ 08541). Military personnel who want to take CLEP should see their education officer or write DANTES, CN, Princeton, NJ 08541.

Many of the tests offered by CLEP are available in two versions: multiple-choice questions only or multiple-choice plus an essay. Some colleges require applicants to take both parts, others just the multiple-choice. CLEP's relevant exam areas are:

- Algebra and Trigonometry
- Analysis and Interpretation
- Calculus and Elementary Functions
- College Algebra
- Computers and Data Processing
- General Mathematics
- Introduction to Management
- Introductory Accounting
- Introductory Business Law
- Introductory Marketing

CLEP tests are given over a two-day period at more than 1,300 centers, most of them on college or university campuses. Each of them sets its own schedule for frequency of testing, so it may pay to "shop around" for convenient dates.

Persons living more than 150 miles from a test center may make special arrangements for the test to be given nearer home. There is a modest charge for this service.

PEP is offered in the state of New York by the Regents College Proficiency Program (7 Columbia Circle, Albany, NY 12203) and everywhere else by the American College Testing Program (P.O. Box 168, Iowa City, IA 52243).

PEP offers exams in these relevant fields:

- Accounting I and II
- Advanced Accounting
- Auditing
- Business Policy
- Corporate Finance
- Cost Accounting
- Federal Income Taxation
- Intermediate Business Law
- Labor Relations
- Management, Human Resources
- Marketing
- Organizational Behavior
- Personnel Administration
- Principles of Management
- Production/Operations Management
- Statistics

PEP tests are given for two consecutive days on a variable schedule in about one hundred locations, nationwide, including most of the Sylvan Learning Centers. Persons living more than 150 miles from a test center may make special arrangements for the test to be given nearer home. There is a modest charge for this service.

CLEP allows exams to be taken every six months; you can take the same PEP exam twice in any twelve-month period.

How hard are these exams?

This is, of course, an extremely subjective question. However, we have heard from a great many readers who have attempted CLEP and PEP exams, and the most common response is, "Gee, that was a lot easier than I had expected." This is especially true of more mature students. The tests are designed for eighteen to twenty-year-olds, and there appears to be a certain amount of factual knowledge, as well as experience in dealing with testing situations, that people acquire in ordinary life situations as they grow older.

Preparing (or cramming) for exams

The testing agencies issue detailed syllabi describing each test and the specific content area it covers. CLEP also sells a book that gives sample questions and answers from each examination.

At least four educational publishers have produced series of books on how to prepare for such exams, often with full-length sample tests. These can be found in the reference section of any good bookstore or library.

Other Examinations

Here are some other examinations that can be used to earn substantial credit toward many nontraditional degree programs.

Graduate Record Examination

The GRE is administered by the Educational Testing Service (P.O. Box 955, Princeton, NJ 08541, (212) 966-5853) and is given at nationwide locations four times each year. There is one general aptitude test and a series of advanced tests designed to test knowledge that would ordinarily be gained by a Bachelor's degree holder in a given field. The exams are available in the following relevant fields:

- Economics
- Mathematics

Schools vary widely in how much credit, if any, they will give for each GRE.

DANTES

The Defense Activity for Non-Traditional Education Support, or DANTES (c/o Educational Testing Service, Rosedale Road, Princeton, NJ 08541), administers its own exams, as well as CLEP and PEP exams. Once given only to active military personnel, DANTES exams are now available to everyone. Tests include:

- Basic Marketing
- Business Law II
- Introductory College Algebra
- Organizational Behavior
- Personnel/Human Resource Management
- Principles of Finance
- Principles of Financial Accounting
- Principles of Statistics

How Life Experience Is Turned into Academic Credit

Many undergraduate distance-learning programs offer a great deal of credit for life-experience learning. MBAs and other business professional degrees tend to be less generous, as the course of study tends to be quite rigid and allows for less creative interpretation. Still, some schools do give life-experience credits for business and professional certifications. If you do hold a diploma in a business field or a professional certification, it's certainly worth asking whether this will be worth any credits, and/or excuse you from any required courses. How do schools decide what's worth what? It isn't easy. Some schools and national organizations are striving toward the creation of extensive "menus" of nontraditional experiences so that anyone doing the same thing would get the same credit.

Credit for Foreign Academic Experience

There are many thousands of universities, colleges, technical schools, institutes, and vocational schools all over the world whose courses are at least the equivalent of work at American universities. In principle, most universities are willing to give credit for work done at schools in other countries, to the same degree that they are willing to accept transfer credits from American schools (yes, a number of schools in this book are non-American, so please forgive us our provincial bias in this section. If you're interested in dealing with, say, an Australian school and have foreign credits, your best bet is to ask the school directly what you need to do in order to get those credits accepted).

Can you imagine the task of an admissions officer faced with the student who presents an advanced diploma from the Wysza Szkola Inzynierska in Poland or the degree of Gakushi from the Matsuyama Shoka Daigaku in Japan? Are these equivalent to a high school diploma, a Doctorate, or something in between?

Until 1974, the U.S. Office of Education offered the service of evaluating educational credentials earned outside the United States and translating them into approximately comparable levels of U.S. achievement. This service is no longer available from the government, which has chosen instead to recognize some private nonprofit organizations that perform the evaluation service.

These services are used mostly by the schools themselves to evaluate applicants from abroad or with foreign credentials, but individuals may deal with them directly.

The costs run from $60 to $150 or more, depending on the complexity of the evaluation. Some of the services are willing to deal with non-school-based experiential learning as well. The services operate quickly; less than two weeks for an evaluation is not unusual. While many schools will accept the recommendations of these services, others will not. Some schools do their own foreign evaluations.

It may be wise, therefore, to determine whether a school or schools in which you have interest will accept the recommendations of such services before you invest in them. As with everything else, shop around, and ask questions to make sure that what you're planning to do will suit your needs.

Typical reports from the services will give the exact U.S. equivalents of non-U.S. work, both in terms of semester units earned and of any degrees or certificates earned. For instance, they would report that the Japanese degree of Gakushi is almost exactly equivalent to the American Bachelor's degree.

It is important to remember that these services are independent, unregulated, and often inconsistent. Work that one agency evaluates as Master's level may be regarded as Bachelor's level (or even less) by another. So if you feel one agency's evaluation is inappropriate, you may wish to try another.

Organizations performing these services include:

Credentials Evaluation Services
P.O. Box 66940
Los Angeles, CA 90066
(310) 390-6276

Educational Credentials Evaluations, Inc.
P.O. Box 92970
Milwaukee, WI 53202-0970
(414) 289-3400

Education Evaluators International, Inc.
P.O. Box 5397
Los Alamitos, CA 90720
(310) 431-2187

International Consultants of Delaware, Inc.
914 Pickett Lane
Newark, DE 19711
(302) 737-8715

International Credentialling Associates, Inc.
150 2nd Avenue N, Suite 1600
St. Petersburg, FL 33707
(813) 821-8852

International Education Research Foundation
P.O. Box 66940
Los Angeles, CA 90066
(310) 390-6276

Joseph Silmy & Associates, Inc.
P.O. Box 248233
Coral Gables, FL 33124
(305) 666-0233

World Education Services
P.O. Box 745, Old Chelsea Station
New York, NY 10113-0745
(212) 966-6311

Correspondence Courses

Appendix C lists 48 schools offering graduate-level courses in MBA-related fields. This may be useful for a couple of reasons. First, some of the schools listed in this book allow students to transfer in prior credits; you may wish to take a few correspondence courses in business administration or related fields before making the big jump to enrolling in an MBA program. In addition, most MBA programs assume a certain baseline knowledge of math, statistics, business concepts, and so forth. You can fill in the gaps with correspondence courses, further ensuring your success when you begin your MBA program. For details, including costs, delivery method (many courses are offered on-line these days, in addition to, or instead of, by traditional correspondence), and requirements, contact the schools directly.

8. Distance-Learning Technologies

When the first distance-learning degree programs debuted back in the 1800s, the technologies involved were pretty simple: pen, paper, postal service. Maybe the occasional telegram if you were really high tech. Now, of course, it's a whole different world. Some prospective distance students, especially those who haven't grown up using computers, may feel a little intimidated by the terminology, or even by the assumption that they need to know about all of this technological stuff. So, for the techno-nervous, two pieces of good news:

1. You may not need to learn about any new technologies. Many programs are still largely based on old-fashioned, traditional book, written assignments, and the like. While computer skills are increasingly required for a number of programs (and in the business world in general), the technophobic will find programs to suit their needs. Marina Bear, wife of one author and mother of the other, earned her accredited Master's degree 100 percent by distance learning, using nothing more high tech than a typewriter and a telephone.

2. Even if you do need to use a computer, it won't be confusing. Really. Trust us on this one. First, as a businessperson, you probably deal with computers every day. If you've somehow managed to avoid developing these skills, it's almost certain that having them will aid your career, perhaps even as much as the degree you bought this book to learn about. In addition, schools have every reason to make their web sites, on-line courses, and other offerings as user-friendly as possible. It's inevitable that more and more programs will develop on-line support and virtual campuses, and will rely on student feedback to make them helpful, informative, and easy to use.

A Few Common Terms Defined:

Traditional Texts: This means pretty much what it sounds like. While schools' definitions of "traditional" may vary, you can basically expect textbook, photocopied or specially printed readings, ring binders of assignments, and the like. A number of schools offer the option of going entirely traditional, or combining media—so you may, for instance, receive a textbook to study, but then get your assignments e-mailed to you.

Video Instruction: This can mean one of a number of things:

Televised instruction: Some local television channels, and one national cable network, offer courses accepted by a number of distance programs. (In some regions, universities broadcast classes over local cable access or public television stations. It's worth investigating whether this is an option in your area.) Knowledge TV, formerly Mind Extension University, is a national private cable system that offers instruction from regionally accredited universities. Subscribers can view courses at will, but to receive credit, they need to be enrolled in a degree program. Electronic University and Connected Education are two companies that manage course delivery with Knowledge TV, mailing out program materials, helping with registration, and so forth.

Videotape instruction: Many programs mail out videotapes to distance students; these are usually just tapes made of on-campus courses, which are sent out once the lecture is completed. Many distance students enjoy this delivery method for a number of reasons: it allows them to feel like they're part of a class, it structures the learning program with regular (usually weekly) deliveries, and it provides them with a library of tapes from which to review and revisit lecture material prior to exams or other assignments.

Compressed video transmissions: It is increasingly common for schools to beam satellite transmissions of lectures to remote locations—usually a corporation, military base, or cooperating university. Students then gather to view the lecture together, and perhaps have discussions or complete tasks as a group.

This was once a one-way street, with the classes simply sent to site, like a TV broadcast. Nowadays, some programs use videoconferencing systems that allow real-time interaction with faculty and on-campus students.

A number of corporate-supported programs now also receive what's called "compressed desktop video," which, as the name implies, can be viewed on a computer with a high-speed Internet connection. During these transmissions, students can ask questions on-line, interact with others, and otherwise participate.

Right now, these methods use technologies not available to the average home-based distance learner, and thus students have to gather at a site that has the needed equipment. As home computers improve and connection speeds get faster, the ideal is to have anyone be able to participate, from anywhere in the world. Stay tuned!

On-line Instruction: Once again, this can mean a wide range of things. The ideal, rarely in place right now, but on the horizon, is a fully interactive Internet-based classroom, where students can take classes in real-time if they desire, or download them for more convenient viewing, interact with each other and with professors, download assignments, browse reference libraries, and take exams. Many schools offer a number of these services, and both the number of providers and usefulness of the technology are growing fast. Here are a few services and terms defined:

Virtual campus: This term means all sorts of things, and you really need to view the campus to know what a school offers. It may simply mean that the school's Internet site offers some basic student services—maybe the opportunity to register for classes and order course materials. Or, it may be a fully interactive site, with student support groups, ongoing web-based classes, and more.

Virtual classroom: An Internet-based course delivery system, almost always presented in real time, usually text (rather than image) based, to allow for students with older, slower modems and computers.

Asynchronous: This means non-real-time connections, such as e-mail, newsgroups, and bulletin boards. Many schools use asynchronous modes of communication, such as having students post comments in a discussion forum or e-mail questions to professors. The advantage of this is that students access information and join ongoing discussions when and where they wish, a major plus for many distance students with hectic work and family schedules, or who may live many time zones away from their schools.

Synchronous: More commonly called live, or real-time. In this mode of connection, students log on and communicate directly on-line. This may be in a chat room, where brainstorming and discussion occurs or, in some programs, in real-time on-line classes or electronic meetings with faculty.

What Methods Are Best for You?

There's really no simple answer. Some distance-learning students like the total independence of working when they like, contacting professors by voice- or e-mail, touching base with others rarely or not at all. Others want or need the structure of weekly meetings, either at distance-learning sites or virtual gatherings on the Internet. As with any continuum, most probably prefer something in between and, indeed, that's what most programs offer. As you read through the listings in chapter 9, you'll find that there's a level of structure and interactivity for just about every need.

9. Schools Offering MBAs and Other Master's-level Business Degrees by Distance Learning

Remember, this chapter lists only schools offering programs with a fairly wide geographic range—either for students anywhere in the world, or at least to students living in a fairly large region. For schools offering distance-learning degrees in a restricted area, check out appendix A. You may well find a school in your area that will serve your needs as well as or better than the schools listed in this section.

The one important thing to bear in mind is that things change. People usually don't think of something like a university moving (but they do), or going out of business (at least one major college or university goes out of business every month on average), or changing its phone numbers (it happens all the time, especially in the US, as new area codes are being added monthly), or even changing its name (such as College of New Jersey becoming Princeton, Kings College becoming Columbia, Queens College becoming Rutgers, and hundreds of other examples).

If a school is listed in the next one hundred pages, but you can't get in touch with them, see Appendix D.

If a school is not listed in the next one hundred pages, and you want to know about them, see Appendix E.

People ask why we don't give tuition figures, and the answer is very simple: these things change so quickly that any information we print will be out-of-date by the time you buy the book, and will only end up annoying someone. Check out a school's web site, or just call and talk to admissions counselors about costs. It really does pay to shop around, as costs vary greatly (as do admissions requirements, amount of work required, and just about every other variable you can imagine).

American College

Richard D. Irwin Graduate School
270 South Bryn Mawr Avenue
Bryn Mawr, PA 19010

Degree awarded:	MS in financial services
Area of concentration:	Financial services
Admissions requirements:	Bachelor's degree
Media:	Traditional texts
Total units in program:	36 credits
Residency:	Two one-week on-campus residencies
Accreditation:	Regional, AACSB
Year founded:	1927
Ownership:	Nonprofit, independent
Phone:	(888) AMERCOLL • (610) 526-1490
Fax:	(610) 526-1465
E-mail:	studentservices@amercoll.edu
Web site:	www.amercoll.edu

American College has been offering business courses via distance learning for 25 years, and awards the degree of Master of Science in financial services (MSFS) to those who complete its 36-credit program. Twenty-four of the credits may be earned off-campus, the remaining 12 are achieved at the school's two required one-week residencies. A graduate certificate is also offered, and is awarded after nine credits are earned.

Individual courses are worth 3 credits each, and students may choose from a list of electives including business valuation, mutual funds, advanced pension and retirement planning, and financial decision making at retirement. On-campus courses completed by each distance student are: communications and research, financial statement analysis, managing the financial services enterprise, ethics and human values, security analysis and portfolio management, and a research project presentation.

Students complete assignments via mailed correspondence lessons, and are encouraged to maintain contact with professors via post, telephone, fax, and e-mail. Classes may be taken separately from the program for graduate credit. Distance learners may use the school's library, advisors, and tutors just like traditional students. A Bachelor's degree is required for admission to the program.

Athabasca University

Public Affairs
1 University Drive
Athabasca, AB T9S 3A3
Canada

Degree awarded:	MBA
Area of concentration:	General business, Information Technology Management, Agriculture
Admissions requirements:	Bachelor's degree plus a minimum of three years of managerial experience, or an acceptable professional designation plus a minimum of five years of managerial experience. Must have a computer and Internet service.
Media:	On-line, software
Total units in program:	12 courses and one applied project
Residency:	One week, plus 2 weekend sessions
Accreditation:	GAAP, AACSB
Year founded:	1970
Ownership:	Nonprofit, independent
Phone:	(780) 675-6100 • (800) 788-9041
Fax:	(780) 459-2093 • (800) 561-4660
E-mail:	auinfo2@athabascau.ca
Web site:	www.athabascau.ca

Athabasca is an open distance-education institution serving more than 10,000 students across Canada; international applicants are welcome in the MBA program. The program requires students to complete twelve courses, two comprehensive examinations, and one applied project. Students are also required to attend one week-long summer school and two additional weekend residencies over the course of the degree program.

Students will normally complete any of the three MBA programs in two-and-a-half to three years. However, school regulations state that students must complete the MBA within six years. A student must successfully complete one course or comprehensive examination in any twelve-month period to maintain active status in the program.

Course materials are delivered via CD-ROM, as well as on-line, and support is available seven days a week. A Lotus Notes-based system allows students to communicate with faculty, share information, and network with others in their study group. Each student is given support and guidance from graduate student advisors, who are available weekdays, weekends, and evenings.

To be admitted, an applicant must have an accredited Bachelor's degree and a minimum of three years of managerial experience, or hold an acceptable professional designation and have at least five years of managerial experience. The GMAT is not required.

Auburn University

Graduate Outreach Program
202 Ramsay Hall
Auburn, AL 36849-5336

Degree awarded:	MBA
Areas of concentration:	Management information systems, finance, healthcare administration, operations management, marketing, human resource management, management of technology
Admissions requirements:	Bachelor's degree, GMAT are required. Courses in calculus, statistics, and word processing are encouraged
Media:	Video and Internet
Total units in program:	60+ quarter hours
Residency:	5 week-long residencies and 1 international trip
Accreditation:	Regional, AACSB
Year founded:	1856
Ownership:	Nonprofit, state
Phone:	(334) 844-4000 • (888) 844-5300
Fax:	(334) 844-2519
E-mail:	jhughes@eng.auburn.edu
Web site:	www.auburn.edu/outreach/dl/

More than 250 professionals in 48 states are currently taking advantage of the distance MBA offered by Auburn University. The program is only available to U.S. residents and overseas students with APO/FPO addresses. Applicants whose native language is not English must prove their proficiency by submitting their scores from the TOEFL (Test of English as a Foreign Language).

Students are expected to have course experience in calculus and statistics, and should have working knowledge of word processing, spreadsheets, and database applications. Coursework for distance learners is offered at the same pace as it is for campus-based students. Each class is videotaped and copies are mailed to distance-learning students. Group discussion and professor contact occur via phone and Internet. Each professor sets up special "office hours" for distance learners, during which they accept phone calls regarding the course of study.

The course requires that at least 60 quarter hours be completed, with a chance of waiving some of the quarter hours for outstanding achievement in undergraduate courses. Sixteen elective hours are required, with 12 of those falling in one of the following areas of concentration: finance, marketing, operations management, management of information systems, management of technology, human resource management, or healthcare management.

The MBA program is generally completed in two-and-a-half years, but Auburn allows students five years to finish. Five week-long residencies and one international trip satisfy the residency requirement for the MBA.

Professional accreditation is from the International Association for Management Education (AACSB).

Ball State University

Graduate Business Programs
Whitinger Building 146
Muncie, IN 47306

Degree awarded:	MBA
Area of concentration:	General business
Admissions requirements:	Bachelor's degree, GMAT, TOEFL (for international students)
Media:	Interactive television
Total units in program:	36-54 credits
Residency:	None
Accreditation:	Regional, AACSB
Year founded:	1918
Ownership:	Nonprofit, state
Phone:	(800) 482 4278 • (765) 285-1931
Fax:	(765) 285-8818
E-mail:	mba@bsu.edu
Web site:	www.bsu.edu/business/mba

Delivery sites are legion for Ball State's MBA program, including locations in Indianapolis, Huntington, Richmond, Upland, Angola, Evansville, and Vincennes. More sites are available in other Indiana towns, as well as in New Jersey and Kentucky, as well as through a wide range of workplaces, high schools, military sites, and hospitals.

The MBA can be completed entirely through interactive satellite television programming. Students watch lessons at one of the delivery sites, and interact with teachers and other students through telephone, mail, fax, e-mail, interactive television, and the World Wide Web.

Services available to distance learners include e-mail, advising and career placement, the campus computer system, and the school library. Distance students may purchase books through the bookstore as well. Students may be asked to have access to the Internet for some classes.

Credits from other institutions may be transferred toward the MBA degree, and students are allowed six years to complete the program. A Bachelor's degree and GMAT scores are required for admission. Foreign students will be asked to submit their scores from the TOEFL.

Bellevue University

1000 Galvin Road South
Bellevue, NE 68005

Degrees awarded:	MBA, Master of Arts in leadership
Areas of concentration:	International business, finance, leadership
Admissions requirements:	Undergraduate degree, any major. Must also have Internet access for on-line courses.
Media:	Web site-mediated classwork, on-line forums, individual and group projects
Total units in program:	36 hours
Residency:	None
Accreditation:	Regional
Year founded:	1966
Ownership:	Nonprofit
Phone:	(402) 293-3702 • (888) 381-8988
Fax:	(402) 293-2020
E-mail:	kconsbru@cccins.gi.cccneb.edu
Web site:	www.bellevue.edu

Bellevue University offers two Master's degrees entirely through on-line courses. Students go on-line to take courses, participate in discussions with professors and fellow students, conduct research at the on-line library, and interact with course advisors. On-line courses are kept small, to encourage an active learning environment. To demo the on-line classroom, go to www.bellevue.edu/online/intro.htm. A seven-minute introductory video is included on-line, and is quite informative, provided you have a fast modem.

Bellevue offers both an MBA and a Master of Arts in leadership through this system. Both consist of 36 course hours and take about 18 months to complete. The programs are designed for a working student with an accredited undergraduate degree and three years of experience in the field. For full admissions requirements, including exams options encompassing the MAT, GMAT or GRE, contact the Director of Graduate Admission, or go to www.bellevue.edu/online/app_process.

Bournemouth University

Talbot Campus
Fern Barrow, Poole
Dorset, BH12 5BB
United Kingdom

Degree awarded:	MBA
Area of concentration:	International tourism
Admissions requirement:	Undergraduate degree
Media:	Multimedia packages involving computer, audio and video technology
Total units in program:	12
Residency:	None
Accreditation:	GAAP
Year founded:	1942
Ownership:	Public
Phone:	(44-1202) 524-111
Fax:	(44-1202) 318-853
E-mail:	studadm@usq.edu.au
Web site:	www.bournemouth.ac.uk and www.usq.edu.au

A joint program with Australia's University of Southern Queensland offers a distance-learning MBA in international tourism. Anyone with an undergraduate degree can enroll, from anywhere in the world. International students register through Queensland; see the web site, above, for more information.

The degree consists of 12 units, usually completed over four years. Each unit is a multimedia package including print, audio, video, computer-managed learning, and electronic communications components. These packages are mailed every semester to students, and include study notes and self-assessment exercises. The recommended load for a part-time student is 2 units per semester.

Grading standards vary from package to package, with basic requirements and deadlines detailed in each. Professors grade, comment on, and return completed coursework to students, and exams are given in various locations around the world—so students can complete the program without ever setting foot on campus.

Some foreign students may find that student support is biased toward Australian students, as most of it comes in the form of Australian libraries, "telephone tutorials," and outreach programs scattered through Queensland and Sydney.

California State University, Dominguez Hills

SAC 2, Room 2126
1000 East Victoria Street
Carson, CA 90747

Degree awarded:	MBA
Area of concentration:	General business
Admissions requirements:	Accredited Bachelor's degree in any field, GMAT (waived with 5 years of experience), computer with Internet connection
Media:	Texts, Internet, some additional readings
Total units in program:	30 units (3 units earned per course)
Residency:	None
Accreditation:	Regional, AACSB, ACBSP
Year founded:	1960
Ownership:	Nonprofit, state
Phone:	(310) 243-2714
Fax:	(310) 516-4178
E-mail:	Internet.mba@soma.csudh.edu
Web site:	som.csudh.edu/Internet.mba

A wholly on-line MBA is available through this state university. The program requires a Bachelor's degree or equivalent in any field, a 2.75 GPA throughout the past 60 semester credits, and a minimum of 450 points on the GMAT. However, the GMAT requirement may be waived if the applicant has an accredited Master's or other advanced degree, a minimum 3.2 GPA on the past 60 credits, or at least five years of verifiable managerial experience. Up to three of the ten courses required for the MBA may be waived if graduate-level business courses have been completed at an accredited university.

Accepted applicants to the MBA program must have a computer with hardware and software meeting the school's requirements, which are listed on the web site. Most of the computer-ware requirements are basic to a decent Internet system, but some specifics include a CD-ROM drive, a SoundBlaster compatible soundcard and microphone, and Microsoft Office 97 productivity suite. Students will be provided an e-mail account by the university.

Students may register for single or double sessions per semester, double being a full load. A dedicated full-time student can expect to earn a degree in nine months. Books are made available at associated university bookstores and the readings are complemented by on-line research. Exams vary depending on the course. Some professors grade solely on the casework completed and others conduct exams live on the Internet.

Capella University

330 2nd Ave South, Suite 550
Minneapolis, MN 55401

Degrees awarded:	MBA, MS in management
Areas of concentration:	General business, management, communications technology
Admissions requirements:	Bachelor's degree, 2.7 GPA
Media:	Internet, interactive CD-ROM
Total units in program:	64 quarter credits for the MBA, 48 quarter credits for the MS in management
Residency:	None
Accreditation:	Regional
Year founded:	1993
Ownership:	Proprietary
Phone:	(612) 339-8650 • (888) CAPELLA
Fax:	(612) 339-8022
E-mail:	mba@tgsa.edu
Web site:	www.capellauniversity.edu

Formerly known as the Graduate School of America, Capella University is a major, well-funded, relatively new institution that offers distance-learning programs via either directed study or the Internet. The directed-study format combines guided independent study and research with minimal residency requirements, including one intensive two-week summer session; the on-line format has no residency component. Both the MBA and the MS in management (with an optional concentration in communications technology) are offered in the on-line format.

The MS and MBA programs give learners a choice in the focus of their program. The MS in management is a shorter, 12-course program, with an emphasis on managerial theory, while the MBA is a 16-course program emphasizing case studies and practical application of management principles.

A recent addition, the e-business concentration focuses on information technology and provides students the opportunity to study online business development, technical infrastructure, and virtual customer bases.

The MS degree is awarded to students who complete twelve on-line courses (48 quarter credits), six from a required list and six from a list of electives. The MBA requires the completion of sixteen on-line courses (64 quarter credits), eleven from a required list and five from a list of electives.

Each on-line course lasts twelve weeks and is made up of eight one-week learning units. The additional time allows for completion of course projects and unfinished work. On-line courses use a discussion group format that requires regular (at least once each week) participation from all learners.

Central Michigan University

Extended Degree Program
Mount Pleasant, MI 48859

Degree awarded:	MS in administration
Areas of concentration:	Various administration and management fields
Admissions requirements:	Bachelor's degree or equivalent, with a GPA of 2.5 overall or 2.7 in the final 60 semester hours of undergraduate study
Media:	Textbooks and study guides
Total units in program:	36 semester hours
Residency:	Attendance at regional off-campus centers
Accreditation:	Regional, AACSB
Year founded:	1892
Ownership:	Nonprofit, state
Phone:	(800) 950-1144
Fax:	(517) 774-2461
E-mail:	celinfo@cmich.edu
Web site:	www.cel.cmich.edu/academics/graduate-degrees.htm#1

Central Michigan University offers a Master of Science in administration, which can be customized with one of seven concentrations: general health services; human resources; international, public, or software engineering; administration; or information resource management. While not fully a distance program, the courses are offered at fifty locations in the United States, Canada, and Mexico. A number of courses are currently offered over the Internet, and plans for more of the degree to go on-line are underway. The Central Michigan MSA is designed to prepare graduates for managerial careers in their current fields, or for transferring their skills to a new career. More than 43,000 students have earned their degrees through CMU's off-campus degree program, and 13,000 are currently enrolled.

Admission requirements are a regionally accredited Bachelor's degree and a GPA of 2.5 overall or 2.7 in the final 60 semester hours of undergraduate study. Learning is administered at one of the fifty learning sites throughout the nation, most being in Michigan, Washington, D.C., Hawaii, the Southeast and the Midwest. Courses at these sites are geared to working professionals, and thus are available evenings or weekends year-round.

All Master's degree programs are operated under the sponsorship of companies, military bases, or professional organizations. In most cases, anyone may enroll, whether or not he or she has an association with the sponsor. If enough applicants from the same city or organization petition the college, Central Michigan may open a learning center in their area. Twenty-one semester hours (of 36 required) must be completed through Central Michigan; up to 10 units may come from prior learning assessment.

Professional accreditation is from the International Association for Management Education (AACSB).

Central Queensland University

Distance Education Centre
Rockhampton M C
Queensland, 4702
Australia

Degree awarded:	MBA
Areas of concentration:	Financial management, general management, human resource management, information systems, international business, management accounting, marketing management, public sector management, tourism
Admissions requirements:	Bachelor's degree in a business field, or a Bachelor's in any field plus two years of managerial experience
Media:	Written modules, Internet and computer software
Total units in program:	12
Residency:	None
Accreditation:	GAAP
Year founded:	1967
Ownership:	State
Phone:	(61-7) 4930-9407
Fax:	(61-7) 4930-9399
E-mail:	ddce-enquiries@cqu.edu.au
Web site:	www.cqu.edu.au

Central Queensland University (CQU) is one of the largest distance education providers in Australia, and welcomes international students. The MBA program offers a number of specializations (financial management, general management, human resource management, information systems, international business, management accounting, marketing management, public sector management, and tourism), or students may choose to do a general program consisting of units from within any or all of these fields.

The MBA consists of 12 units, which, on a part-time basis, normally constitute 2 course credits per unit. A student taking 4 units per term is considered full-time. CQU also has a four-term operating year, which gives students the option of fast-tracking their studies and completing the MBA even sooner, finishing in about one year. Course materials are provided in a number of ways, most commonly written modules mailed between the school and students. Interactive technology is also increasing rapidly at CQU and many units are now offered via software, or over the Internet.

Applicants should have a Bachelor's degree (or equivalent) in business, management, commerce, or economics, or a Bachelor's in any field plus either a graduate diploma in business or management, or two years of work experience in a managerial field. Most courses do not require final exams; for those that do, the school operates almost 1,000 exam centers worldwide, to serve the needs of distance students.

Distance-learning materials are published at the college, and the school's distance-learning newsletter, Insideout, may be ordered from the web site. The web site itself is a bit challenging to negotiate, with specific information about programs offered being somewhat hard to find.

Charles Sturt University

School of Business
Locked Bag 767
Wagga Wagga 2678
Australia

Degree awarded:	MBA
Areas of concentration:	General business
Admissions requirements:	Undergraduate degree or equivalent
Media:	Internet
Total units in program:	12 subjects
Residency:	None
Accreditation:	GAAP
Year founded:	1989
Ownership:	Public
Phone:	(069) 33 2756
Fax:	(069) 33 2930
E-mail:	admissions@csu.edu.au
Web site:	www.csu.edu.au/study/de.html

One of several business degrees available via the Internet from Charles Sturt (see web site for complete details), the MBA program is designed to give students knowledge in a broad variety of subjects including accounting, economics, finance, management, marketing, and strategic planning. Students will be expected to demonstrate analytical and problem solving skills through work with case studies and assignments focusing on managerial problems.

Applicants are normally required to have an undergraduate degree from a recognized Australian tertiary institution or a qualification deemed to be equivalent. Applicants with other academic or professional qualifications or work experience acceptable to the university will be considered.

The course consists of 12 subjects, six of which are core subjects and six elective. The electives are grouped into the following specializations: Human Resources Management, Industrial Relations, Strategic Management, Total Quality Management, Finance, Public Sector Management, Marketing, International Marketing, Management of Organizational Change, and Training & Development. Students may follow one of the specializations or may choose a variety of subjects from any of the electives. A Graduate Certificate is available for students who choose to study a total of 4 subjects, and students who leave the program after completing 8 of the subjects are rewarded a Graduate Diploma.

City University

335 116th Avenue SE
Bellevue, WA 98004

Degree awarded:	MBA
Areas of concentration:	General business, information systems, financial management, personal financial planning, individualized study, managerial leadership, marketing
Admissions requirements:	Bachelor's degree, any field
Media:	E-mail, traditional methods
Total units in program:	45 credits
Residency:	None
Accreditation:	Regional, AACSB
Year founded:	1973
Ownership:	Nonprofit, independent
Phone:	(425) 637-1010 • (800) 426-5596
Fax:	(425) 637-9689
E-mail:	info@cityu.edu
Web site:	www.cityu.edu

City University offers a distance-learning MBA in general business, or in a number of specializations, including information systems, financial management, personal financial planning, individualized study, managerial leadership, and marketing. The school's web site states that at City, "the world is your campus," and learning methods include on-line courses, e-mail, traditional correspondence, and more. In addition to fully distance methods, the school also offers its MBA in a classroom format through teaching locations in Washington state, California, British Columbia, Switzerland, Germany, and Slovakia.

The university is in the process of developing extensive on-line services. Already, students can take courses, access university information, register, and communicate with faculty members and advisors on-line. Additional programs are to be added soon, and as a bonus, the web site is very user-friendly.

Class materials may be purchased at the bookstore, located in Renton, Washington, or ordered over the telephone.

Clarkson College

101 South 42nd St.
Omaha, NE 68131-2739

Degree awarded:	MS in management
Area of concentration:	Management
Admissions requirements:	Call for requirements
Media:	Video and audio, e-mail, and Internet
Total units in program:	45 credit hours
Residency:	None
Accreditation:	Regional
Year founded:	1888
Ownership:	Nonprofit, independent
Phone:	(402) 552-3041 • (800) 647-5500 (ext. 23037 for Coordinator of Distance Education)
Fax:	(402) 552-6057
E-mail:	admiss@clrkcol.crhsnet.edu
Web site:	www.clarksoncollege.edu

Clarkson's Masters programs include an MS in management (with a concentration in business), which may be earned entirely through distance learning. Using tele-conferencing, e-mail, Internet, video and audiocassettes, and fax, students can confer with the faculty, be involved in roundtable discussions, and receive feedback about their progress. In order to be enrolled in distance education, a student must live at least one hundred miles from Omaha, Nebraska.

Applicants are encouraged to call the Coordinator of Distance Education at the toll-free number for current enrollment requirements. The Coordinator can also advise students concerning the transfer of course work and the awarding of advanced placement credit or evaluative credit, all of which may reduce the number of hours needed to complete a degree and reduce the total tuition cost for completing the degree requirements.

Clarkson College distance education students are required to have Internet access with an e-mail account in their own name, an answering machine or service on a home telephone, a VCR, an audio tape player that will also record, and access to a fax machine. Specific programs may require additional equipment. An e-mail is sent from the student to the Coordinator by the second week of the semester to verify that the student is "complying" with the equipment standards. Grave repercussions follow those students who fail to comply, including being dismissed from the program, loss of financial aid, and possibly "a grade of WF," according to the web site.

College for Financial Planning

6161 South Syracuse Way
Greenwood Village, CO 80111-4707

Degree awarded:	MS in financial planning
Area of concentration:	Financial planning
Admissions requirements:	Bachelor's degree in business-related major
Media:	Traditional text, e-mail, World Wide Web
Total units in program:	36 credit hours
Residency:	None
Accreditation:	Regional
Year founded:	1972
Ownership:	Proprietary
Phone:	(303) 220-1200 • (800) 237-9990
Fax:	(303) 220-4941
Web site:	www.fp.edu

The Master's degree program at the College for Financial Planning awards students a Master of Science (MS) degree and provides graduate-level study in five areas: financial planning, wealth management, tax planning, retirement planning, and estate planning. Students combine financial planning concepts and techniques presented in previous courses in a final capstone course. This course provides a comprehensive client scenario, including background information and client goals.

Students keep tabs on their progress by taking self-administered exams throughout their course of study. The MS is awarded to students who successfully complete 36 credit hours under the program. Up to 6 credits may be transferred in from another institution toward the student's total, subject to approval by the college.

Students can take advantage of faculty counseling via telephone, regular mail, fax, or e-mail. The college's web site provides detailed course information, including current study materials, frequently asked questions, and a sample of course projects. Through the Learning Resource Center (LRC) of the University of Phoenix (owned by the same parent company), students have access to several searchable databases; articles and abstracts may be available on-line, through local libraries, or from the LRC for a charge.

Courses are taken via the Internet, using e-mail and the World Wide Web for instruction and assignments.

College of Estate Management

Whiteknights
Berkshire
Reading RG6 6AW
United Kingdom

Degree awarded:	MBA
Areas of concentration:	Construction and real estate
Admissions requirements:	Bachelor's degree and/or professional qualifications plus 3 years experience
Media:	Written materials, audio- and videocassettes
Total units in program:	13 courses
Residency:	Two workshops per year on campus, one on-campus exam
Accreditation:	GAAP
Year founded:	1919
Ownership:	Independent
Phone:	(44-118) 986-1101
Fax:	(44-118) 975-5344
E-mail:	info@cem.ac.uk
Web site:	www.cem.ac.uk

The MBA program at the College of Estate Management is designed to reinforce existing management skills and develop new areas of expertise within the construction and real estate industries. Students take a look at corporate business administration at the highest level, with an emphasis on construction and real estate development.

The full program is three years by distance learning with workshop-seminars held twice a year, in spring and fall, at locations in the UK, Singapore, Malaysia, and Hong Kong. Examinations are held annually in June. Participants should expect to spend at least 10 hours a week on their studies over 40 weeks in the first two years, and 12 hours a week over 40 weeks in the third year, which includes writing a dissertation.

A Bachelor's degree and/or professional qualification plus at least 3 years post-qualification experience is required for admittance to the program. Applications to join the course should reach the college by July 1 in order to start the course in September of that year.

Colorado State University

Colorado Distance Degree Program
Spruce Hall
Fort Collins, CO 80523-1040

Degree awarded:	MBA
Areas of concentration:	General business, with a focus on IT and globalization
Admissions requirements:	Bachelor's degree, GMAT may be waived with 8 years of work experience.
Media:	Software, e-mail
Total units in program:	36 credits
Residency:	None
Accreditation:	Regional, AACSB
Year founded:	1870
Ownership:	Nonprofit, state
Phone:	(970) 491-5288 • (800) 491-4MBA, ext. 1
Fax:	(970) 491-2348
E-mail:	bizdist@lamar.colostate.edu
Web site:	www.biz.colostate.edu

The MBA program at Colorado State continues the school's long-standing tradition of distance education. The University was the first to establish a video-based degree program in 1967. The curriculum focuses on the broad function of business operations, with specific emphasis on team building, information technology, and globalization.

The GMAT is required, although this requirement may be waived if the applicant has a minimum of eight years of full-time work experience and a cumulative GPA of at least 3.0 on a 4.0 scale. Meeting the minimum requirements does not guarantee a waiver of the GMAT. The MBA program is 36 credits. Students are not required to complete a final examination or professional paper in order to graduate.

All business courses use an electronic communications software product called "embanet." The software allows communication with faculty, staff, and students; posting of class materials; group work; and real-time chats. The college pays for the embanet software for each student. Distance degree students are responsible for their own Internet access.

Students may register by fax or mail. The program is available to students in the U.S. and Canada, as well as those with APO or FPO addresses.

Dalhousie University

School of Business Administration
6152 Coburg Road
Halifax, NS B3H 3J5
Canada

Degree awarded:	MBA
Area of concentration:	Financial services
Admissions requirements:	Bachelor's degree or 5 years of relevant management experience, Institute of Canadian Bankers–approved courses, and letters of reference
Media:	Traditional texts
Total units in program:	16 5-credit courses
Residency:	Intensive sessions at various locations, as well as one-week "capstone course" at Dalhousie
Accreditation:	GAAP
Year founded:	1818
Ownership:	Provincial
Phone:	(902) 494-1378 • (800) 205-7510
Fax:	(902) 494-5164
E-mail:	mbush@mgmt.dal.ca
Web site:	mbafs.mgmt.dal.ca

Through its School of Business Administration, Dalhousie University offers an MBA with a focus in financial services, in partnership with the Institute of Canadian Bankers. Designed for managers in the financial services industry, the courses are taught through a combination of distance study and intensive sessions held at various off-campus locations. The degree may be earned through part-time study, geared to the needs of the fully employed.

Once accepted by Dalhousie University, a student must complete the requirements for the MBA degree within seven years. Sixteen 5-credit graduate level courses are required to fulfill the degree, including seven courses offered by The Institute of Canadian Bankers, and nine courses provided by Dalhousie University's School of Business Administration.

Eight of the nine courses are offered via a distance-education format consisting of 17 weeks of distance study and assignments, followed by a three-day intensive learning session. These sessions are held in Toronto, Vancouver, and various Caribbean locations. The "capstone course" is a one-week intensive learning session conducted at the university, after eight weeks of distance-learning preparation.

Deakin University

Graduate School
Faculty of Business and Law
Geelong VIC 3217
Australia

Degree awarded:	MBA
Areas of concentration:	General business, accounting and finance, arts and entertainment management, economics, education, electronic commerce, human resource management, international business, law, leadership and communication, marketing, public management, strategy and planning
Admissions requirements:	Bachelor's degree or equivalent, two years work experience, or completion of the Graduate Certificate of Management or Graduate Diploma of Business Administration (see below)
Media:	Traditional text
Total units in program:	12 units
Residency:	Several five-day residencies
Accreditation:	GAAP
Year founded:	1974
Ownership:	Public
Phone:	(61 3) 5227 2216
Fax:	(61 3) 5227 2655
E-mail:	gsm-enquiries@deakin.deu.au
Web site:	www.deakin.edu.au

The Deakin MBA promises to develop a capacity for "dealing with the totality of an organisation's management," according to the web site for this Australian university. The program emphasizes the creative, analytical, and interpersonal elements of business leadership. Several five-day residential units are held on Deakins' Geelong campus, and exams are administered throughout Australia and in other locations, where feasible.

The distance version of the Deakin MBA mirrors the residential program, with 12 units required for the degree. A Graduate Certificate of Management is awarded for those who complete 4 units of the 12, and after 8 units are completed a Graduate Diploma of Business Administration is available. Students who have completed postgraduate studies in management or have earned their CPA may be eligible for credit toward the MBA.

Students may choose to study for a general business MBA, or can strike a path in one of several interesting focus areas, including arts and entertainment management, electronic commerce, and law. Study materials are mailed to students, and are divided into study guides (which include general information, questions on the material), readers (collections of other writings relevant to the study guides), and textbooks. Some textbooks may be ordered online with free shipping.

Drexel University

3141 Chestnut St.
Philadelphia, PA 19104

Degree awarded:	MBA
Areas of concentration:	General business
Admissions requirements:	Home computer with Internet access, email account, Java-capable browser, transcripts, two letters of recommendation, bachelor's degree, GMAT, essay.
Media:	Internet, electronic bulletin board system, traditional texts
Total units in program:	21 classes
Residency:	Three on-campus weekends
Accreditation:	Regional, AACSB
Year founded:	1891
Ownership:	Private
Phone:	(800) 2-DREXEL, (215) 895-2111 (Business School)
E-mail:	admissions@drexel.edu
Web site:	http://mbaonline.lebow.drexel.edu

Distance students at Drexel University may earn their MBA through Internet study. Seven foundation classes and 14 advanced classes comprise the course of study to earn the degree. The entire program may be completed in as little as 21 months. The online MBA program follows a cohort model for the advanced classes, with groups of students taking the same 14 courses at the same time throughout their studies.

Three on-campus residencies are required for MBA distance students, at the beginning, middle-point, and end of the advanced class program. These residencies are structured as concentrated workshop weekends, and include on-campus components that continue online throughout each quarter of study. Foundation classes require no residency.

While the cohort groups complete each class in time with one another, individual students within cohorts choose when to study each week: real-time classwork is not part of the online program. Students order their textbooks from Drexel's homepage and discuss assignments via electronic bulletin board. Registration and exams are handled online, and students have access to technology hotlines via Drexel's business associate, eCollege.com.

Duke University

The Fuqua School of Business
Box 90127
Durham, NC 27708-0127

Degree awarded:	MBA
Area of concentration:	Global management
Admissions requirements:	Bachelor's degree, eight years of managerial experience
Media:	Internet
Total units in program:	15 courses
Residency:	Five two-week sessions at one of the extension campuses
Accreditation:	Regional, AACSB
Year founded:	1838
Ownership:	Nonprofit, independent
Phone:	(919) 660-7804 • (800) 372-3932
Fax:	(919) 660-8044
E-mail:	fuqua-gemba@mail.duke.edu
Web site:	www.fuqua.duke.edu

Duke's Global Executive MBA program is a 19-month program designed for experienced managers who want to learn more about global management. It combines five 2-week residential sessions at sites in Europe, Asia and the Americas with continuing distance education using a wide range of interactive communication tools. The majority of learning is done over the Internet. In addition to using bulletin boards and e-mail for case discussion, students use multimedia lesson plans and web pages, among other methods, to communicate, research and learn. The American contact for the program is Lisa Lee at the Fuqua School of Business.

In order to be accepted to the program, applicants must hold a Bachelor's degree and have at least eight years of managerial experience. The ideal applicant is an executive who currently holds a global management position in his or her corporation, or who plans to do so in the near future. Five two-week sessions satisfy the residency requirements for the program; these are held at locations in North America, Europe, Asia, and South America.

Edith Cowan University

External Studies
P.O. Box 830
Claremont, WA 6010
Australia

Degree awarded:	MBA
Area of concentration:	General business
Admissions requirements:	Bachelor's degree
Media:	Various, mostly text-based
Residency:	None
Accreditation:	GAAP
Year founded:	1990
Ownership:	Private
Phone:	(61-9) 273-8500
Fax:	(61-9) 442-1330
E-mail:	extstudi@echidna.cowan.edu.au
Web site:	www.cowan.edu.au/homepage.html

This Australian university offers many degrees through distance learning, including an MBA to students worldwide. Learning methods vary, but can involve a combination of workbooks and study guides, additional readings, audio-visual materials, and other instructional media. In addition, students may be directed to obtain and read various necessary texts and journal articles. Formerly known as the Western Australian College of Advanced Education.

Empire State College

Office of Graduate Studies
28 Union Avenue
Saratoga Springs, NY 12866

Degree awarded:	MBA
Area of concentration:	General business
Admissions requirements:	Bachelor's degree from a regionally accredited college or university, courses in accounting, economics, and statistics, computer and Internet literacy
Media:	Internet, independent study
Total units in program:	60 credit hours
Residency:	Two (2–3 day) weekend residencies in New York state per year (total of no more than 5)
Accreditation:	Regional
Year founded:	1971
Ownership:	Nonprofit, state
Phone:	(877) YOUR-MBA (968-7622)
Fax:	N/A
E-mail:	MBA@sescva.esc.edu
Web site:	www.esc.edu/MBA

A part of the State University of New York (SUNY) system, Empire State offers an MBA that allows distance learners to combine a generous amount of credit for prior learning with Internet-based courses, independent study, and several weekend seminars held in New York state.

A competency-based program, this MBA lets you test out of 28 of the 60 credits required through assessment of prior knowledge, including workplace training and managerial experience. Up to 12 credits can also come from other accredited graduate programs. Focused on management skills, the coursework is divided into three key themes: ethics, globalization, and organization effectiveness.

Students take Internet-based classes, and complete additional work through guided independent study, with a faculty mentor providing support and guidance in both prior learning assessment and program issues.

Applicants should have a Bachelor's degree from an accredited university or college, and have taken 3 credits of accounting, 6 credits of economics (micro- and macro-), and 3 credits of statistics. Applicants should also possess computer and Internet literacy.

Florida Gulf Coast University

Distance Learning Program
10501 FGCU Boulevard
Fort Myers, FL 33908-4500

Degree awarded:	MBA
Areas of concentration:	Accounting, banking, computer information systems, entrepreneurship, finance, general management, health administration, human resources, manufacturing and operations systems, marketing, and others
Admissions requirements:	Bachelor's degree, GMAT
Media:	Texts, e-mail or regular post
Total units in program:	54-57
Residency:	None
Accreditation:	Regional
Year founded:	1997
Ownership:	State
Phone:	(941) 590-2315
Fax:	(941) 590-2310
E-mail:	tdugas@fgcu.edu
Web site:	www.fgcu.edu

Applicants to the Florida Gulf Coast MBA program must have earned an accredited undergraduate degree, have maintained a 3.0 GPA in upper division coursework and have a score of 500 on the GMAT. Prior to admission into the program, students may complete a maximum of 9 semester hours of courses toward their MBA.

The program is divided into 24 semester hours of foundation courses, 12 semester hours of required core courses, 12 semester hours of concentration courses and 6 to 9 hours of elective courses. Students who have completed undergraduate courses in business may receive course waivers for foundation courses. Without waivers, program length varies from 54 to 57 hours. A traditional Master's degree normally takes between one and two years to complete, while part-time learners usually take at least three to four years.

Textbooks for distance learners may be purchased over the telephone or via e-mail, and are shipped via UPS. Course outlines are available on the web site, or a printed copy can be mailed from the school.

Performance is evaluated by papers and projects that are submitted electronically or by regular mail. In some cases, on-line exams will be offered and in others, proctored exams will be arranged in the student's area. Should distance learners care to visit the campus, all services and facilities are open to them just as they are to on-campus students. Financial aid and scholarships are also available to distance learners.

Georgia Southern University

MBA Program
P.O. Box 8125
Statesboro, GA 30460-8125

Degree awarded:	MBA
Areas of concentration:	General business
Admissions requirements:	GMAT, transcripts, 2+ years work experience, TOEFL for international students
Media:	Not yet determined, refer to the web site
Total units in program:	Not yet determined, see web site
Residency:	Not yet determined, see web site
Accreditation:	Regional, AACSB
Year founded:	1906
Ownership:	Nonprofit, state
Phone:	(912) 681-5767
Fax:	N/A
E-mail:	mba@gasou.edu
Web site:	http://www2.gasou.edu/mba/webmba.htm

The Georgia Southern University MBA program is in process. The following material is quoted from Georgia Southern University's web page:

"On May 16, 1999, representatives from six AACSB accredited universities in Georgia (Augusta State, Georgia College, Kennesaw, Valdosta, West Georgia and GSU) met regarding a proposal to jointly offer an MBA program on the web. Each of the six schools will develop and teach three courses—one in the prerequisite category and two in the 7000-level category. GSU will tentatively be responsible for delivering Fundamentals of Management and Marketing, International Business, and an Information Technology course focusing on ERP/SAP.

"Even though the Web MBA is still in the pre-approval stages and the graduate faculties of all six schools will have to endorse the program, we hope to be up and running January 2000. Student admissions requirements for GSU student applicants will be as follows: Must be admitted to GSU's MBA program, must validate that they have access to an adequate computer and file server, must attend a one-day orientation, must have minimum of two years experience in full-time/ professional work. Drop-ins must meet the requirements and be approved by Dr. J. Michael McDonald, Director, COBA Office of Graduate Studies."

Henley Management College

Greenlands
Henley-on-Thames
Oxfordshire, RG9 3AU
United Kingdom

Degree awarded:	MBA
Areas of concentration:	General business, project management
Admissions requirements:	Bachelor's degree, three to five years of relevant experience, minimum age of 27
Media:	Lotus Notes, texts, CD-ROM
Total units in program:	10 courses, including dissertation
Residency:	Three-day residential at start of program, series of 2-day workshops subsequently
Accreditation:	GAAP, AACSB
Year founded:	1945
Ownership:	Private
Phone:	(44-1491) 571-454
Fax:	(44-1491) 418-861
E-mail:	mba@henleymc.ac.uk
Web site:	www.henleymc.ac.uk

Henley currently serves around 7,000 distance-learning MBA and diploma students in over 80 countries. Applicants for the MBA are required to be at least 27 years old, have a Bachelor's degree from a recognized university, and have three to five years of relevant business/managerial experience. Students lacking the academic qualifications can be admitted to the Diploma in Management program, which represents the first two parts of the distance-learning MBA. After completing this, they can progress to the MBA if they wish.

Henley has associates in more than 20 countries who provide local support, tutoring, and workshops. Elsewhere (including in the USA), students can join what the school calls its "International Stream," which allows them to consolidate workshop attendance into one-week blocks. All students, wherever they are located, may take advantage of electronic support via Lotus Notes, which they can access 24 hours a day. Printed texts, audio and videocassettes, and CD-ROMs are also used to deliver materials.

Distance learners should expect to complete their degree in about three years. They may apply at any time, with courses beginning in January, April, August, and October of every year. The MBA program consists of three parts; there is an assignment due at the end of each subject, and an examination at the end of each part. A final dissertation of 15,000 words is also required.

Heriot-Watt University

U.S. Agent: Financial Times Management, Inc.
Two World Trade Center, Suite 1700
New York, New York 10048

Degree Awarded:	MBA
Area of concentration:	General business
Admissions requirements:	None
Media:	Traditional texts
Total units in program:	36
Residency:	None
Accreditation:	GAAP
Year founded:	1821
Ownership:	State
Phone:	(212) 390-5030 • (800) 622-9661
Fax:	(212) 344-3469
E-mail:	info@hwmba.net
Web site:	www.hwmba.edu

With more than 8,000 students in over 120 countries (including more than 4,000 in the United States and Canada), Heriot-Watt's MBA program is by far the largest in the world. The only requirement for earning the degree is passing nine rigorous three-hour exams, one for each of the required nine courses (marketing, economics, accounting, finance, strategic planning, etc.). The exams are given twice a year on hundreds of college campuses worldwide (some 100 in the United States and Canada).

Students buy the courses one or more at a time, as they are ready for them. The courses consist of looseleaf textbooks (average: 500 pages) written by prominent professors specifically for this program. Courses are not interactive: there are no papers to write, quizzes or other assignments, and no thesis. Each course averages about 160 hours of study time. The entire MBA can be completed in one year, although 18 to 36 months is more common.

Heriot-Watt University has a 350-acre campus in Edinburgh, Scotland, with more than 10,000 on-campus students pursuing Bachelor's, Master's and Doctorate degrees in many scientific, technical, and business fields. Only the MBA and several highly technical Master's degrees (acoustical science, vibration studies, construction management) can be earned by distance learning.

Hong Kong Baptist University

School of Continuing Education
224 Waterloo Road
Au Shu Hung Garden Terrace
Kowloon, Hong Kong
Peoples Republic of China

Degree awarded:	MBA
Area of concentration:	General business
Admissions requirements:	Bachelor's degree, GMAT, 2 years work experience
Media:	Internet
Total units in program:	60
Residency:	None
Accreditation:	GAAP
Year founded:	1990
Ownership:	Private
Phone:	(852) 2339-5435
Fax:	(852) 2339-5444
E-mail:	sce@hkbu.edu.hk
Web site:	www.strath.ac.uk • www.hkbu.edu.hk/~sce/

The MBA offered by Hong Kong Baptist is offered jointly with the venerable University of Strathclyde in Scotland. Distance studies are administered out of Hong Kong but are identical to the coursework studied by residential students in the UK. Applicants should possess a Bachelor's degree from a recognized university or comparable institution, have at least two years of relevant work experience, and have passed the GMAT. Appropriately qualified applicants are interviewed to establish motivation, maturity, communication skills, language proficiency, and suitability for the course. Applicants without a degree but with strong professional credentials and at least five years of relevant experience may be admitted to the Diploma in Business Administration program and, once they successfully complete this, may be admitted to the MBA.

The 60-credit MBA consists of three main elements: foundation classes, electives, and the final project. Students generally complete the entire program within a two-and-a-half-year period, but the time can be as short as two years or as long as six.

Indiana University

Kelley Direct Online Consortium MBA Program Office
Graduate School of Business
801 W. Michigan St.
Indianapolis, IN 46202

Degree awarded:	MBA
Areas of concentration:	General business
Admissions requirements:	Employer must join partnership with Kelley, Bachelor's degree, GMAT scores
Media:	Internet
Total units in program:	48 semester hours
Residency:	Four 5-day residencies in Indianapolis
Accreditation:	Regional, AACSB
Year founded:	1969
Ownership:	Nonprofit, state
Phone:	(317) 278-1566
Fax:	(317) 274-7301
E-mail:	CMBA@iupui.edu
Web site:	http://bus.iupui.edu/cmba/index.html

Indiana University's Kelley School of Business offers a consortium-based MBA program for distance students. To take advantage of the program, a student's employer must join the Kelley Direct OnLine Consortium. Companies interested in becoming a member of the consortium should contact program coordinator Andrea Fagan via phone at (812) 855-8674, or via e-mail at anfagan@indiana.edu.

The first year of this 24-month program is spent covering the foundations of business theory and practice. The second year allows students to sharpen their focus through electives, although students are allowed five years in which to complete the 48 semester hours required for the MBA. Outside coursework may be applied toward the degree, per approval. Distance students have access to campus career counseling and placement, financial aid, the library, advising, e-mail and computer accounts, election to Beta Gamma Sigma (a business honor society), and the school's magazine, Business Horizons.

Coursework is divided into the categories of accounting, business law, economics, finance, management, marketing, operations, and technologies. Most of the coursework is completed online, but students must attend four 5-day residencies in Indianapolis, one for each of the quarters.

Institute for Financial Management

Manchester Business School &
University of Wales, Bangor
Bangor, Gwynedd, LL57 2DG Wales
United Kingdom

Degree awarded:	MBA
Areas of concentration:	Financial management and financial services
Admissions requirements:	Undergraduate degree, three or more years of work experience
Media:	Traditional texts mailed between school and student
Total units in program:	8 core modules (4 on accelerated program), plus 4 electives (3 on AP)
Residency:	Two annual 6-day sessions
Accreditation:	GAAP
Year founded:	
Ownership:	Nonprofit, state
Phone:	(44-1248) 371-408
Fax:	(44-1248) 370-769
E-mail:	R.Henry@bangor.ac.uk
Web site:	www.ifm.bangor.ac.uk

This MBA program is delivered jointly by the Manchester Business School and the School of Accounting, Banking, and Economics at University of Wales, Bangor. With a concentration in financial management and financial services, it is designed specifically for financial managers, accountants looking to broaden their financial knowledge, and other finance sector professionals. Applicants holding certain professional credentials (chartered accountants, etc.) may be eligible for the accelerated program, in which 5 of the 12 required modules can be waived.

Course delivery is accomplished via a combination of distance learning and two annual 6-day residencies, held both in the UK and at various centers worldwide. These residential workshops are interactive and case-study-based, and form a vital part of the program. Individual students are permitted to vary their program schedules to meet the demands of their specific professional and personal needs.

To be accepted, applicants must have an undergraduate degree and a minimum of three years of work experience.

The basic program consists of 8 core modules (covering basics such as finance and accounting, marketing, managerial economics, organizational behavior, and strategic management) and 4 electives. Accelerated students take 4 core courses and 3 electives.

ISIM University

501 South Cherry Street
Room 350 – Admissions Office
Denver, CO 80246

Degrees awarded:	MBA, MS in information management or information technology
Area of concentration:	Information resources management
Admissions requirements:	Bachelor's degree, resume demonstrating professional accomplishments, goals statement, transcripts, three letters of recommendation
Media:	Internet, capstone project
Total units in program:	36
Residency:	None
Accreditation:	DETC
Year founded:	1987
Ownership:	Proprietary
Phone:	(303) 333-4224 • (800) 441-ISIM (4746)
Fax:	(303) 336-1144
E-mail:	admissions@isimu.edu
Web site:	www.isimu.edu

This school offers an M.S. in information management or information technology, and MBA education takes place via ISIM's "electronic campus," instructor-guided learning that uses the school's interactive virtual classroom, accessible through the Internet.

ISIM has won numerous awards from the United States Distance Learning Association (USDLA) for their graduate degree courses.

ISIM requires the following items for admission into their programs: a Bachelor's degree from an accredited or state-approved institution, a resume demonstrating professional accomplishments, a goals statement, transcripts indicating under-graduate and/or postgraduate work, three letters of recommendation, and a seventy-five-dollar application fee.

A maximum of 15 credits out of a total of 36 can be earned through a combination of transfer credits, credit by exam, or prior experience. Transfer credits can be accepted from an accredited institution. A capstone project is required of every stu-dent. The average student takes two years to complete either of the programs.

Foreign students are admitted, and no financial aid is available.

Accreditation is from the Distance Education and Training Council.

Jones International University

9697 East Mineral Ave.
Englewood, CO 80112

Degrees awarded:	MBA, MA in business communication
Areas of concentration:	Business communication, e-commerce, global enterprise management, health care management, entrepreneurship, information technology, negotiation and conflict, and project management
Admissions requirements:	Bachelor's degree, transcripts, 2.5 GPA or above, one year of work experience, three letters of recommendation, resume, goals statement, TOEFL for international students
Media:	Internet
Total units in program:	42 credit hours for the MBA, 35 for the MA
Residency:	None
Accreditation:	Regional
Year founded:	1995
Ownership:	Private
Phone:	(303) 784-8045 • (800) 811-5663
Fax:	(303) 784-8547
E-mail:	info@international.edu
Web site:	www.international.edu

In 1999, Jones International University became the first fully online university—meaning there is no physical campus for students; all coursework is exchanged over the Internet—to receive accreditation from one of the six regional accrediting agencies (North Central Association).

Jones International University began offering graduate courses leading to an MA in business communication in 1995. In 2000 JUI introduced an MBA degree. Products of a technology-driven school, both degrees focus on the importance of emerging technologies in today's business world. Specialization options in the MBA program include e-commerce and information technology management.

The curriculum consists of weekly modules sent and returned over the Internet, with two types of faculty interacting with the students and their work. Known as "content experts," one set of JIU faculty crafts the coursework and grades the students based on the established criteria. The rest are called "teaching faculty," instructors who present the material to students and interact with them directly via the computer system. Courses begin each month on a 16-week or more accelerated 8-week term. Designed for the working, time-starved professional, access to coursework and resources such as the online library is 24/7.

Jones International University was formerly known as International University, which in turn was originally International University College.

Keller Graduate School of Management

One Tower Lane
Oakbrook Terrace, IL 60181-4624

Degree awarded:	MBA, several others (see below)
Areas of concentration:	General management, accounting, finance, health services, human resources, information systems, international business, marketing, project management, telecommunications management
Admissions requirements:	Bachelors degree, transcripts, GMAT or GRE scores, interview, home computer with Internet access
Media:	Internet, videocassettes, email
Total units in program:	52-64 credit hours
Residency:	None
Accreditation:	Regional, AACSB
Year founded:	1973
Ownership:	Nonprofit, private
Phone:	(630) 571-1818
Fax:	(630) 571-2350
E-mail:	sbranick@keller.edu
Web site:	www.keller.edu

Several Master's level degrees are available through Keller. Alongside the MBA, the school offers the following: Master of Accounting and Financial Management, Master of Human Resource Management, Master of Information Systems Management, Master of Project Management, and Master of Telecommunications Management. Coursework is handled via e-mail and bulletin board postings, videocassettes, and the World Wide Web. Distance learning students read course materials, write papers, conduct applied research and take exams, all online.

The School's online site, http://online.keller.edu, offers course syllabi and assignments, Keller's online library, and other Web-based resources. CD-ROM companion disks and online lecture notes are also available through the site. Distance students have online access to career counseling, academic advising, and financial aid information. Texts and course materials are available through Keller's online bookstore.

Academic performance is assessed via evaluation of contributions to team/group activities, participation in threaded discussions and performance on individual assignments, projects, papers and case studies. Quizzes and exams are also heavily integrated into the program.

Keller also offers a Saturday MBA program through its centers in Illinois, Indiana, Wisconsin, Missouri, Virginia, Georgia, Florida, Nevada, and California.

Kettering University

Office of Graduate Studies
1700 West Third Avenue
Flint, MI 48504-4898

Degree awarded:	MS in business
Area of concentration:	General business
Admissions requirements:	Bachelor's degree, GMAT, letter of recommendation, and essay
Media:	Videocassettes and traditional texts
Total units in program:	54 credits
Residency:	None
Accreditation:	Regional, ACBSP
Year founded:	1919
Ownership:	Nonprofit, independent
Phone:	(810) 762-7494
Fax:	(810) 762-9935
E-mail:	gradoff@kettering.edu
Web site:	www.gmi.edu

Originally established as the General Motors Institute, Kettering offers its Master of Science (MS) program through videotapes at over 100 remote sites and will also mail the tapes to the students' places of work once the employer has entered into a corporate partnership. Regular classes are recorded at the University and sent, along with paperwork, to distance students, who follow along with the same schedule of tests and assignments expected of the traditional students. Occasionally, Internet access is required for some of the courses.

Interaction between students and professors is through mail, fax, e-mail, and telephone. Special office hours are held by professors for the sole purpose of fielding calls from students. Distance learners are eligible for financial aid, and also have access to the school's library and academic advising services.

Successful applicants will hold a Bachelor's degree, and must submit GMAT scores, a letter of recommendation, and an essay of intent. A total of 54 credits are required for the degree. Assignments are completed and mailed to professors, and tests may be arranged at one of the remote sites or at corporate partner locations.

Lehigh University

Office of Distance Education
205 Johnson Hall
36 University Drive
Bethlehem, PA 18015

Degree awarded:	MBA
Area of concentration:	General business
Admissions requirements:	Bachelor's degree, transcripts, GMAT, letter of recommendation, essay
Media:	Teleconferencing, mail, telephone, fax, e-mail, and computer
Total units in program:	30 credits
Residency:	One or two days
Accreditation:	Regional, AACSB
Year founded:	1865
Ownership:	Independent, nonprofit
Phone:	(610) 758-6210
Fax:	(610) 758-6269
E-mail:	mak5@lehigh.edu
Web site:	www.lehigh.edu/~indis/indis.html

Lehigh's MBA is offered through a program that is, at present, available only to corporate-sponsored groups, allowing full-time working professionals to continue an education with only a brief visit to campus. (Two courses require attendance, which totals one or two Saturdays at the school.) Corporations participating in the program include 3M, DuPont, Merck, Bristol-Meyers Squibb, Ortho, Allied Signal, and many more.

Admissions requirements include a Bachelor's degree, GMAT scores, a letter of recommendation, and an essay of intent. Also, of course, one's employer must be willing to participate in the program.

Classes are delivered nationwide via live satellite broadcast, and students can interact in real-time by 24-line audio bridge, fax, or an on-line message center, called the "electronic whiteboard." Students have access to the library, computer system and school-sponsored chat rooms. A total of 30 credits are earned in the program, of which a maximum of 6 may be earned from outside experience.

Professional accreditation is from the International Association for Management Education (AACSB).

Lesley College

School of Management
29 Everett Street
Cambridge, MA 02138

Degree awarded:	MS in management
Area of concentration:	Management
Admissions requirements:	Bachelor's degree, essay of intent, letter of recommendation, work experience, and resume
Media:	Interactive television and World Wide Web
Total units in program:	40 semester credits
Residency:	None
Accreditation:	Regional
Year founded:	1909
Ownership:	Nonprofit, independent
Phone:	(617) 349-8675
Fax:	(617) 349-8678
E-mail:	cmpd@mail.lesley.edu
Web site:	www.lesley.edu/som.html

Lesley College's off-campus Master of Science (MS) program offers the same line of study as its on-campus counterpart. However, the components of the program may be tailored to meet the particular needs and schedules of the students and participating organizations. By using interactive television and the World Wide Web, Lesley broadcasts its management courses to off-site locations at schools, community centers, and corporations. Currently, regional sites operate throughout Massachusetts as well as Vermont, New Hampshire and Maine. National sites operate in Colorado, Idaho, Missouri, Montana, Nebraska, Nevada, South Carolina, Washington, Wisconsin, and Wyoming.

Lesley will open a new site if there is sufficient interest in the program. Students do not have to wait until the beginning of a traditional semester to begin their degree program. Once a group of 20 to 25 students—the approximate number needed to offer a program—have applied, a Lesley site coordinator who lives in the area notifies students of the start-up dates and the location of the facility where weekly classes will be held. The site coordinator is also responsible for the general administration of the program at the site, to include registering students, ordering textbooks, arranging for classroom space, distributing course schedules and information and acting as a liaison with Lesley faculty and administrators.

Students interact with professors via teleconferencing, fax, telephone, and e-mail. It may be necessary for students to have Internet access for some of Lesley's programming. Distance learners have access to Lesley's library, bookstore, and academic advising.

Liberty University

1971 University Blvd.
Lynchburg, VA 24502

Degree awarded:	MBA
Areas of concentration:	General Business
Admissions requirements:	Bachelor's degree, GPA of 3.0 or higher, three letters of recommendation, accounting and business coursework experience, GMAT, computer with Internet access, applicants should be 25 or older
Media:	Videocassettes and traditional texts
Total units in program:	36 hours
Residency:	None
Accreditation:	Regional
Year founded:	1971
Ownership:	Church
Phone:	(804) 582-7763 • (800) 424-9595
Fax:	(800) 628-7977
E-mail:	flking@liberty.edu
Web site:	www.liberty.edu

Coursework is sent to students on videocassette for review. Online study guides are available for reference. Students are given 120 days to complete each of the courses, with writing assignments. Most students average around five courses per year. The 36-hour MBA program is usually completed in about two-and-a-half years, although five years are allowed for completion. The courses are also available on a course-by-course basis for students who don't want to complete the full program.

Liberty assumes that incoming students have had academic or work experience relating to business and accounting. Core courses offered cover topics such as managerial finance, corporate responsibility, and global economic environment alongside more basic organizational and marketing theories. Elective courses delve into human resources management, entrepreneurial ventures, and executive communication.

Master's level coursework is transferable from approved graduate schools, and life experience may count toward course credit. Liberty is a Christian school, and states as its mission "to produce Christ-centered men and women with the values, knowledge, and skills required to impact tomorrow's world." Distance students should be at least 25 years old before applying to the program.

Madonna University

School of Business
Cohort Online Programs
36600 Schoolcraft Road
Livonia, MI 48150

Degree awarded:	MS in business administration
Areas of concentration:	Quality and operations management, international studies
Admissions requirements:	Bachelor's degree, high GPA or GMAT, essay of intent, work experience
Media:	Video and audio, Internet
Total units in program:	36 semester hours
Residency:	None
Accreditation:	Regional, AACSB
Year founded:	1947
Ownership:	Church
Phone:	(734) 432-5354 • (800) 852 4951
Fax:	(734) 432-5393
E-mail:	neuhause@smpt.munet.edu
Web site:	www.munet.edu

Madonna University offers a Master of Science in Business Administration (MSBA) to 25 students at a time through its cohort program. Coursework is delivered to students worldwide at their homes or workplaces via video and audio-cassettes, on-line conferencing, e-mail, and the World Wide Web. Students are required to have a computer with Internet access, and interaction between students and professors is generally through the Internet.

A Bachelor's degree, GMAT scores (if GPA is below 3.25), an essay of intent, and previous work experience are required of applicants to this 36-semester-hour program. The MSBA is a relatively short program, with a maximum time allowance of 22 months to complete. Distance students enjoy access to the school's library, book-store, and academic advisors. Credits may be transferred from other institutions, and may also be earned through military and business training.

Two branches of specialization may be followed on the path to the MSBA degree. The quality and operations management specialization instructs students in the basics of business ethics, behavior, and leadership, and then includes a large research segment on quality, taking into account technology, culture, the individual, and groups. International studies specialists focus on trade, marketing, and economics, and must fulfill a foreign business and cultural experience requirement, earned by overseas business experience.

Marylhurst University

Graduate Department of Management
P.O. Box 261
17600 Pacific Highway (Hwy. 43)
Marylhurst, OR 97036

Degree awarded:	MBA
Area of concentration:	General business
Admissions requirements:	Bachelor's degree, GMAT, essay, letter of recommendation, previous work experience
Media:	World Wide Web
Total units in program:	60 quarter hours
Residency:	None
Accreditation:	Regional
Year founded:	1893
Ownership:	Church
Phone:	(503) 699-6246
Fax:	(503) 636-9526
E-mail:	kpaul@marylhurst.edu
Web site:	www.marylhurst.edu

The MBA program at Marylhurst is designed for working professionals who already have a reasonable amount of experience in the business world; the average age of incoming students is 35.

The MBA is awarded after students complete the required 60 quarter hours, including a business plan and an end-of-degree project. Coursework focuses on the building blocks of business: accounting, information, finance, marketing, human capital, communication, and strategy. The expanding global marketplace is explored, and students are instructed in how to form effective working relationships through team-based problem solving. Students must complete the program within five years.

Marylhurst's program is competency-based. At the beginning of the program, students undergo assessment to make sure they have a grasp of business basics; midway through the program, a business plan is drawn up and graded; and at the end, they are assessed on the basis of a practicum, project, or internship.

All learning is done via the World Wide Web, and students are required to have a computer with Internet access, Windows 95, and a 14.4K or better modem. Library, bookstore, and advising services are available to distance students.

Morehead State University

College of Business
Combs 214
Morehead, KY 40351

Degree Awarded:	MBA
Areas of concentration:	Bank management, computer information systems, human resource management, health care administration
Admissions requirements:	Bachelor's degree
Media:	Internet, audio, and video
Total units in program:	36 semester hours for business majors, 50 for others
Residency:	None
Accreditation:	Regional, AACSB, ACBSP
Year founded:	1922
Ownership:	Nonprofit, state
Phone:	(606) 783-2183
Fax:	(606) 783-5025
E-mail:	msu-mba@morehead-st.edu
Web site:	www.morehead-st.edu

Morehead's MBA program is designed for students who have completed an undergraduate degree in any field, although those whose degrees are in a business-related field may complete the MBA in a minimum of 36 semester hours, as compared to 50 hours for those with degrees in other areas. The new nonresident "manager-friendly, schedule-friendly" program offers classes over the Internet as well as via two-way interactive audio/video at a variety of sites in the eastern Kentucky service area. The Internet courses can, of course, be accessed from anywhere. Courses are offered evenings, weekends and Saturdays, on an 18-month rotation.

Coursework is mailed to students' homes or may be obtained at several campuses and substations throughout Kentucky, including Eastern and Northern Kentucky universities, three off-campus centers, and several high schools and middle schools. School benefits extended to distance learners include library and campus computer use, e-mail, tutoring, advising, and career search facilities.

The degree can be a general MBA, or students can choose to specialize in bank management, computer information systems, human resource management, or health care administration.

Morehead is a candidate for professional accreditation from the International Association for Management Education (AACSB).

Napier Univeristy

Business School
MBA Programme
New Craig
Craighouse Campus
Craighouse Road
Edinburgh, EH10 5LG
Scotland

Degree awarded:	MBA
Area of concentration:	International business
Admissions requirements:	Bachelor's degree of sufficient caliber, and managerial experience
Media:	Text and Internet
Total units in program:	
Residency:	Two workshops per year
Accreditation:	GAAP
Year founded:	1964
Ownership:	Public
Phone:	(44-131) 455-5016 / 5009
Fax:	(44-131) 455-5041
E-mail:	s.ferrier@napier.ac.uk
Web site:	www.napier.ac.uk

Edinburgh's third-oldest university offers both "open" and "distance" learning MBA programs, geared mainly to managers operating in the UK and internationally. Students are expected to continue with their full-time employment, and the school stresses that they must work hard to earn the MBA. Open learning students have regular study weekends on-campus, while distance students attend workshops twice a year. The admissions process is rigorous, designed to select only those applicants with sufficient academic and professional qualifications, as well as sufficient business experience. Learning takes place through printed correspondence texts, e-mail tutoring, various Internet functions, and by telephone.

This MBA program is the product of several European schools and is designed as an MBA for U.K. and international markets. For more information, potential students are encouraged to contact Mrs. Sheila Ferrier, Course Administrator, at the numbers and address above.

National University

11255 North Torrey Pines Road
La Jolla, CA 92037

Degree awarded:	MBA
Area of concentration:	General business
Admissions requirements:	Bachelor's degree, 2.5 GPA
Media:	Video, CD-ROM, Internet
Total units in program:	60
Residency:	3 courses on campus
Accreditation:	Regional, AACSB
Year founded:	1971
Ownership:	Nonprofit, independent
Phone:	(619) 642-8212
Fax:	(619) 642-8709
E-mail:	pmontroy@nunic.nu.edu
Web site:	www.nu.edu

National University's Global MBA requires students to be on campus for the final three courses of a 60-unit program. Forty-five units must be earned through the program; the remainder may be transferred or earned through outside experience. Applicants must have a Bachelor's degree and a 2.5 GPA on previous work.

The GMBA is a twelve-course program divided into three modules. Each course must be completed within two months, and students can take up to two courses at a time. Coursework is delivered to the students through a variety of media, including videocassettes, closed circuit television, CD-ROM, the Internet, and e-mail. Students must have access to a computer, and the school will transmit materials to distance learners at their homes, offices, or military bases.

School benefits extended to distance learners include access to NU's library, computer system, and advisors.

New York Institute of Technology

Room 417, Theobald Hall
P.O. Box 8000
Old Westbury, NY 11568

Degree awarded:	MBA
Area of concentration:	General business
Admissions requirements:	Bachelor's degree, GMAT, essay
Media:	Internet, interactive audio and video
Total units in program:	
Residency:	None
Accreditation:	Regional, AACSB
Year founded:	1955
Ownership:	Nonprofit, independent
Phone:	(516) 686-7516 • (800) 345-NYIT
Fax:	(516) 626-6830
E-mail:	spender@admin.nyit.edu
Web site:	www.nyit.edu

NYIT offers a web-based MBA to students through its extensive distance-learning program. Students from around the world have used the program to gain their degrees. A fiber-optics system provides two-way interactive audio and video between NYIT's three campuses. The system is connected to the local Board of Cooperative Educational Services and the 126 public schools systems they serve. The system combines two-way video/audio, audio graphics, computer conferencing, and Internet services.

The relatively new on-line MBA program provides an opportunity for students to interact and exchange ideas among themselves and with experienced, professional faculty members who bring reality and real-world applications to each class. It follows more than ten years of NYIT's success with distance degrees for undergraduates. Students begin their learning with an overview of the business world, focusing on aspects such as information systems, marketing and finance, managing new products, system hardware and software and comparative economic systems. A bachelor's degree in any field, GMAT scores, and an essay of intent are required for admission to the program. For a full curriculum, contact Dean J.C. Spender, School of Management, (516) 686-7423, spender@admin.nyit.edu.

Northeastern Illinois University

5500 N. Saint Louis Ave.
Chicago, IL 60625

Degree awarded:	MBA
Area of concentration:	Accounting, Finance
Admissions requirements:	GMAT, Bachelor's degree
Media:	Traditional mixed with extracurricular experience
Total units in program:	48 for second majors, 60 for business majors
Residency:	Some
Accreditation:	Regional, AACSB
Year founded:	1867
Ownership:	Nonprofit, state
Phone:	(773) 794-5247
Fax:	(773) 794-6246
E-mail:	jm-behncke@neiu.edu
Web site:	www.neiu.edu

The two programs offered by NIU give students a broad, interdisciplinary orientation to modern business theory and practice. Both general business majors and nonmajors study each facet of business toward their individual degrees. This program is especially helpful for those who may wish to start or work in a small- or medium-sized enterprise where employees and managers will be required to exhibit a broad range of business competencies. The General Business Administration degree has two options, MBA for second majors and MBA for business majors.

The second major option is designed for students who wish to specialize in a specific field and combine their knowledge with business. A language student may choose to use this program for international business, for example. There are 48 credits involved in the degree. The general business administration option requires 60 credits.

NIU is currently offering classes through two programs, the Board of Governor's Bachelor of Arts Degree Program and the University Without Walls program. The programs are loose in definition, advising students to report on their learning, both of classroom materials (which are mailed to the students) and their outside experience. Students write papers each semester describing what they have learned, and grades are based upon these papers. It is possible that in the future certain aspects of these two systems may be incorporated into the MBA programs above. For more information, contact the school at webteam@neiu.edu or call (773) 583-4050.

Nottingham Trent University Law School

Burton Street
Belgrave Centre
Nottingham NG1 4BU
United Kingdom

Degree awarded:	MBA
Area of concentration:	Legal practice
Admissions requirements:	Five years of work experience, references
Media:	Traditional texts, off-site experience
Total units in program:	8 modules
Residency:	Three 4-day intensive weekends
Accreditation:	GAAP
Year founded:	1945
Ownership:	Private
Phone:	(44-115) 948-6085
Fax:	(44-115) 948-6569
E-mail:	marketing@ntu.ac.uk
Web site:	www.ntu.ac.uk

Nottingham Law School, the largest university law school in the UK, offers an MBA with a concentration in legal practice. The degree requires eight intensive study weekends. The program is tailored to students who already have knowledge in the fields of law and business and are seeking further legal education.

MBA applicants should have at least five years experience in a law office. The degree is ideal for lawyers and senior management professionals with functional management responsibilities, and applies the management principles and techniques taught in business school to the world of law.

The program is delivered through a series of intensively taught short residential modules, a project, and an ongoing program of personal development. A series of on-campus sessions are held, taking students through three four-day weekends of learning. Also included in the program are an overseas (outside the U.K.) consultancy and an off-site management project. These are designed to test students' knowledge in real work situations. Student progress is based on written reports and a final dissertation.

All courses are open to applicants from the U.K. and overseas.

Nova Southeastern University

Virtual MBA Program
3100 SW 9th Street
Ft. Lauderdale, FL 33315

Degree awarded:	MBA
Area of concentration:	General business
Admissions requirements:	Bachelor's degree with 2.5 GPA
Media:	Internet
Total units in program:	41 hours
Residency:	One week (optional)
Accreditation:	Regional, AACSB
Year founded:	1964
Ownership:	Independent, nonprofit
Phone:	(954) 262-5059 • (800) 672-7223, ext. 5059
Fax:	(954) 262-3822
E-mail:	vmba@sbe.nova.edu
Web site:	www.sbe.nova.edu/omba

Nova Southeastern University's School of Business and Entrepreneurship introduced on-line courses in January 1998, starting with prerequisite courses for many of its Master's programs. By that summer, the school's Virtual MBA was available to students. The Virtual MBA program is designed to be completed entirely on-line, with the exception of a values integration workshop, offered at various times throughout the year on campus in a one-week format. Students may opt to satisfy this requirement by completing a final project instead, making the program wholly distant.

In Nova's on-line courses, instructors use e-mail, bulletin boards, and chat rooms to facilitate question-and-answer sessions with students and to receive and return homework assignments. Each on-line course is limited to approximately 10 students. A course begins with an e-mail introduction from the professor. Students then submit a short biography explaining their interest in the course. The instructor responds with a short syllabus, a schedule of homework assignments, and a schedule of any preassigned communication times. Coursework can be done on virtually any type of Pentium-based computer with at least Windows 95 and the Office 97 software suite. Instructors may include on-line video clips.

Courses can include three basic types of communication: person-to-person e-mail; electronic bulletin boards for asynchronous communication over a designated period of hours or days; and chat rooms for synchronous communication at specific times.

Ohio University

College of Business
Copeland Hall
Athens, OH 45701-2979

Degree awarded:	MBA
Area of concentration:	General business
Admissions requirements:	Bachelor's degree, 2 to 4 years of work experience
Media:	Internet
Total units in program:	9
Residency:	Some
Accreditation:	Regional, AACSB
Year founded:	1804
Ownership:	State
Phone:	(740) 593-20721 • (800) 622-3124
Fax:	(740) 593-0319
E-mail:	milter@ohiou.edu
Web site:	mbawb.cob.ohiou.edu

This largely distance-learning program is designed for working professionals, allowing them to integrate on-the-job experiences into the learning process. A degree is earned in two years. There are three one-week residencies, one each at the beginning, middle, and end of the program. There are also three required weekend stays each year on the campus, spaced every 3 months. The academic program is structured around nine learning projects, each targeted at specific learning outcomes.

Participants use the "MBA Without Boundaries" Intranet to access learning modules and do individual research, to collaborate with other members of their learning team, and to interact with faculty. They work collaboratively on learning projects using the databases and software provided by the school, which allows real-time meetings, virtual office hours with faculty, and electronic tutorials to assist with the specific skills needed to solve particular problems.

During the residencies, participants concentrate on the specific goals of the current project, address content modules on related topics, and participate in workshops that focus on the development of leadership skills. Workshop topics include "Selling Your Self and Your Ideas," "Creativity and Ideation," "Team Building," "Decision Making," "Negotiation," and "Career Development and Personal Learning."

Professional accreditation is from the International Association for Management Education (AACSB).

Oklahoma State University

College of Business Administration
201 Business Building
Stillwater, OK 74078

Degrees awarded:	MBA, MS in telecommunications management
Areas of concentration:	General business, telecommunications management
Admissions requirements:	Bachelor's degree, 3.4 GPA, GMAT
Media:	Video, texts
Total units in program:	50 credit hours
Residency:	None
Accreditation:	Regional, AACSB
Year founded:	1890
Ownership:	Nonprofit, state
Phone:	(405) 744-4048
Fax:	(405) 744-6143
E-mail:	cba_info@okway.okstate.edu
Web site:	www.bus.okstate.edu

An MBA and an MS in telecommunications management are provided via two-way video to participating corporate sites. Topics for videos include financial accounting, management of information systems and customer analysis. Faculty assign texts for each class and point students to specific questions asked on the web site. Students write papers based on the discussions and on the essay questions from the web site, and then fax, e-mail or send papers in to the instructor via FedEx.

Alongside the papers, midterm and final exams are graded in each class. Twelve core classes, a practicum and several electives round out an MBA.

Students are expected to have earned a Bachelor's degree for the course and a working knowledge of business is helpful, but no previous work experience is necessary. A GPA of 3.4 and GMAT scores are also used as criteria for admission to the program.

Old Dominion University

MBA Program
Hampton Boulevard
Norfolk, VA 23529

Degree awarded: MBA
Area of concentration: General business
Admissions requirements: Bachelor's degree, GMAT, essay, letter of recommendation
Media: Television
Total units in program: 49 credit hours
Residency: None
Accreditation: Regional, AACSB
Year founded: 1930
Ownership: Nonprofit, state
Phone: (757) 683-3163
Fax: (757) 683-4505
E-mail: admit@odu.edu
Web site: web.odu.edu

Courses for the MBA program at Old Dominion are delivered to workplaces, military bases, or other participating schools. Classes may also be taken at off-site centers as arranged by the university. Instruction comes in the form of television programs. Students interact with classmates and professors via television, videoconferencing, e-mail, fax, and the World Wide Web. Access to the Internet is required for some courses.

To be accepted to the program, students must have a Bachelor's degree, GMAT scores, and one or more letters of recommendation. An essay of intent is also required of all applicants. The 49 credits in the program must be completed within six years, although most students do so in much less time.

Distance learners enjoy access to the school's library and computer system, as well as e-mail, advising, and the campus bookstore. Credits may be transferred from other schools, and may be earned through exams and portfolio assessment. Financial aid is available to distance students.

Open University of Hong Kong

30 Good Shepherd Street
Ho Man Tin
Kowloon, Hong Kong

Degree awarded:	MBA
Area of concentration:	General business
Admissions requirements:	A recognized degree in a business-related field or a professional qualification equivalent to a degree, two or more years of business experience. May be waived with a certificate from the school (see below).
Media:	Texts mailed to students, audio- and videocassette
Total units in program:	60
Residency:	None
Accreditation:	GAAP
Year founded:	1989
Ownership:	State
Phone:	(852) 2768-6000
Fax:	(852) 2761-3935
E-mail:	regwww@.ouhk.edu.hk
Web site:	www.ouhk.edu.hk

This school was originally created to serve Hong Kong students, but it is expanding into the rest of China, and eventually plans to enroll students from other parts of the world. Accredited by the Hong Kong Council for Academic Accreditation, the school offers a number of Bachelor's and Master's programs via distance learning. Through a combination of transfer credits, comprehensive self-study packs and supplementary audio-visual materials, students learn without direct interaction with the school. In some cases tutorials are arranged, but they are not required, and may be subject to geographic limitations.

While exams are generally administered at the Hong Kong campus, arrangements can be made to take them elsewhere. The school was modeled on the Open University in England, and some of that school's course materials are offered through the Hong Kong program. The majority of the instruction is in English, although an increasing number of programs are available in Chinese. This school was formerly known as the Open Learning Institute of Hong Kong.

Admission requirements include a business-related Bachelor's degree and two years of work experience. This requirement may be waived if the student has completed a Post-Graduate Certificate in Business Administration or equivalent.

Open University of the Netherlands

Euro-MBA Desk
Faculty of Business and Public Administration
Valkenburgerweg 167
NL - 6419 AT Heerlen
The Netherlands

Degree awarded:	MBA
Area of concentration:	European business
Admissions requirements:	Bachelor's degree, fluency in English, three years of work experience
Media:	Texts and multimedia
Total units in program:	14 units
Residency:	Some
Accreditation:	GAAP
Year founded:	1984
Ownership:	State
Phone:	(31-45) 576-2404
Fax:	(31-45) 576-2103
E-mail:	information@euromba.org
Web site:	www.euromba.org

The Netherlands's first nontraditional university offers its Euro-MBA in the English language. The Euro-MBA program focuses on European business and management, using modern distance-learning methods in combination with intensive residential weeks. Distance-learning courseware and electronic tutoring facilities take up more than 50% of the program, enabling students to combine studying with a full-time job. Students are obliged to attend 6 residential weeks in 6 different parts of Europe over a period of 2 years, write a Master's thesis, and collaborate on a consultancy report with a multicultural team.

The program is open to professionals who have at least three years of work experience, who are fluent in English, and who have a Bachelor's degree or equivalent. Students can enter the program three times a year: in September, January, and May.

Members of the European Association of Distance Teaching Universities have developed a second program, called the European Law Program. It is a postgraduate course of study intended for graduates or students in the final stages of their Master's program.

All exams take place in the Netherlands.

Open University

Business School
Walton Hall
Milton Keynes, Buckinghamshire, MK7 6AA
England

Degree awarded:	MBA
Area of concentration:	General business
Admissions requirements:	Bachelor's degree
Media:	Text, audio, video, software, e-mail and Internet
Total units in program:	One 12-month and four 6-month courses
Residency:	Some
Accreditation:	GAAP, AACSB
Year founded:	1969
Ownership:	Nonprofit, state
Phone:	(44-1908) 653-449
Fax:	(44-1908) 653-744
E-mail:	CREL-GEN@open.ac.uk
Web site:	oubs.open.ac.uk

Established in 1969, the Open University is now the largest distance-learning institution in the world. Students study in their own homes and on their own schedules, using a combination of correspondence texts and audio- and videocassettes, software and e-mail, or, increasingly, the Internet. Some courses have week-long summer schools or weekend residential schools, and some require that the applicant be a resident of the UK or other European country. Credit is earned through a combination of continuous assessment and passing the course examination.

The school is linked with many universities and programs throughout Europe and is also actively involved in establishing a presence in the US, including seeking regional accreditation. It prides itself on giving people a second chance when they've been turned down by other schools.

Open University brought its degree programs to North America in 1999, in association with Western Governors University.

Oxford Brookes University

School of Business
Wheatley Campus
Oxford, OX33 1HX
England

Degree awarded:	MBA
Areas of concentration:	General business, education
Admissions requirements:	Bachelor's degree and work experience
Media:	Text, audio, video, computer conferencing, study groups
Total units in program:	15
Residency:	Some courses may require residency
Accreditation:	GAAP
Year founded:	1970
Ownership:	State
Phone:	(44-1865) 485-962
Fax:	(44-1865) 485-830
E-mail:	mba-bus@brookes.ac.uk
Web site:	www.brookes.ac.uk

The distance MBA program at Oxford Brookes University is conducted over two years of open-learning study. All students take the same set of courses, and are assessed through the same processes. All courses commence in September, and the open-learning course may also recruit students at other points in the year. Some residency may be required.

Entry criteria include a requirement that the candidate has completed at least three years of relevant managerial or professional experience.

Pace University

Director, Online Executive MBA Program
Lubin School of Business
Pace University
One Pace Plaza
New York, NY 10038-1598

Degree awarded:	MBA
Area of concentration:	General business
Admissions requirements:	Application, resume, transcripts, letters of recommendation, computer literacy statement, interview, $60 non-refundable fee
Media:	Internet, group projects during residencies
Total units in program:	9 projects
Residency:	9 weekend residencies
Accreditation:	Regional, AACSB
Year founded:	1906
Ownership:	Independent, nonprofit
Phone:	(212) 346-1833
Fax:	(212) 346-1933
E-mail:	e.MBA@PACE.edu
Web site:	http://www.lubin.pace.edu/e.mba/index.html

Pace's program combines online-supported learning with nine residencies, totaling 28 days over a two year period. Students work in cohorts on nine large-scale projects and learning exercises, each focusing on complex business issues. Working independently, each student completes a tenth project that focuses on a strategic issue facing his or her employer.

Residency weekends are held at the completion of each project. During the residency periods student teams present their projects to both program faculty and practitioner experts. Students also complete assessment exercises and attend managerial skill workshops. A significant portion of each residency period is devoted to developing the next project.

Aside from the school's application, applicants to the MBA program are required to submit their current resume, transcripts, letters of recommendation, a computer literacy statement. An interview is also required. Credits from other MBA programs are not eligible for transfer toward credit in the Pace program.

Residencies are held at one of Pace's Manhattan campuses. Faculty for the distance MBA program are all full-time faculty members of the Pace University Lubin School of Business.

Portland State University

Statewide MBA Program
P.O. Box 751
Portland, OR 97207-0751

Degree awarded:	MBA
Area of concentration:	General business
Admissions requirements:	Bachelor's degree, GMAT
Media:	Videocassettes, telephone, Internet, videoconferencing
Total units in program:	72
Residency:	Twice-annual Saturday sessions
Accreditation:	Regional, AACSB
Year founded:	1988
Ownership:	Nonprofit, state
Phone:	(503) 725-4822 • (800)547-8887, ext. 4822
Fax:	(503) 725-5525
E-mail:	askadm@osa.pdx.edu
Web site:	www.swmba.pdx.edu

PSU's School of Extended Studies in collaboration with the School of Business Administration offers the "Statewide MBA" through a number of colleges, community colleges, local businesses, and corporate sites throughout Oregon and southwestern Washington state.

Classes generally meet two evenings a week, and students must also get involved in project teams with others at their site. One week after each lecture is delivered on-campus, Statewide MBA students view that class on videotape. There is a toll-free number for students to use to communicate with faculty concerning coursework. Web sites are available for each course and contain course materials and places for students to interact with each other and with the faculty.

A total of 72 credit hours are required to complete the degree. Of the 72 credit hours, a 49-credit hour core integrates management and the functional business areas with a focus on competing in a global economy. The remaining 23 credit hours provide 6 credits in current business issues and applied project learning and 17 credits of focused preparation courses. Up to 12 credits may be waived through a successful petition of the faculty or by passing relevant exams.

Qualified applicants will have a Bachelor's degree and a GMAT score of 470 or higher. The program takes three years to complete (with a maximum of seven allowed), and all students must go to the PSU campus twice a year for a Saturday program.

Professional accreditation is from the International Association for Management Education (AACSB).

Purdue University

Krannert School of Management
1310 Krannert Executive Center
West Lafayette, IN 47907-1310

Degree Awarded:	MBA
Areas of concentration:	General business, management, agribusiness
Admissions requirements:	Bachelor's degree, 3.0 GPA, GMAT
Media:	Internet, text
Total units in program:	48
Residency:	Varies
Accreditation:	Regional, AACSB
Year founded:	1869
Ownership:	Nonprofit, state
Phone:	(765) 494-7700
Fax:	(765) 496-3483
E-mail:	webmaster@mgmt.purdue.edu
Web site:	www.mgmt.purdue.edu/

The web site at Krannert advertises four executive MBA programs. The Executive Master's in Management Program (EMS) is a two-year program. Off-campus assignments are completed and six two-week residencies take place during the program, with a two-week international trip finishing the degree. The International Master's in Management Program (IMM) is a residency program with classes split between Indiana, Hungary and Holland. The Executive Master's in Management Weekend Program is a Saturday-only course that meets for three years and is designed with commuters in mind. The Executive MBA in agribusiness is a two-year program that combines distance-learning technology with four two-week residencies, one of which will be an international location.

Courses are split into three modules, each module containing 16 credits. Specific assignments vary, but include Internet projects and traditional texts. Applicants should have a Bachelor's degree, sufficient GMAT scores, and a GPA of 3.0 or higher.

Professional accreditation is from the International Association for Management Education (AACSB).

Ramkhamhaeng University

Huamark
Bangkapi
Bangkok, 10240
Thailand

Degree awarded:	MBA
Area of concentration:	General business
Admissions requirements:	Entrance examination
Media:	Text, satellite TV, audio, video, Internet, CD-ROM, radio
Total units in program:	48 credits
Residency:	None
Accreditation:	GAAP
Year founded:	1971
Ownership:	Nonprofit, state
Phone:	(66-2) 318-0867
Fax:	(66-2) 318-0917
E-mail:	admin@ram1.ru.ac.th
Web site:	www.ru.ac.th

With over 400,000 students, Ramkhamhaeng, which operates on the open-admissions system, is one of the world's largest universities. They currently have over 300,000 distance-learning students, including 1,800 MBA students.

Coursework is delivered via printed correspondence materials, satellite teleconferencing, audio- and videocassettes, the Internet, CD-ROM, and radio and TV broadcasts. RU has cooperative arrangements with the University of Pittsburgh, Kansas State, Northrop University, the University of Missouri-St. Louis, and Pittsburgh State, among others. All course materials are in Thai, as is the distance-learning portion of the web site.

Regent University

School of Business
1000 Regent University Drive
Virginia Beach, VA 23464

Degrees awarded:	MBA, MA in management
Areas of concentration:	General business, management
Admissions requirements:	Bachelor's degree, letter of recommendation, resume
Media:	Traditional texts, video- and audiocassettes, Internet
Total units in program:	30 for MA, 57 for MBA
Residency:	Two five-day sessions are required for both degrees
Accreditation:	Regional
Year founded:	1977
Ownership:	Nonprofit
Phone:	(800) 373-5504
Fax:	(757) 579-4369
E-mail:	tomstan@regent.edu
Web site:	www.regent.edu/distance

The MBA and MA in management can be earned through a combination of correspondence courses, guided independent study, audio- and videocassettes, and instruction by telephone and mail, plus a total of two one-week periods on campus. An accelerated program allows students who have completed three years of undergraduate work (90 semester hours) and have five years of work experience to enroll in the Master's program without completing a Bachelor's degree. Owned by Pat Robertson, this university integrates traditional Judeo-Christian ethical principles in the teaching of each course.

Students are required to have a computer with access to the Internet for part of the program. Access to a VCR is also required. Interaction between students and professors is accomplished through face-to-face meetings, audioconferencing, post, telephone, or e-mail. Access to the school bookstore, academic advising, and career placement services are all provided to distance students. In addition, some courses require distance students to work with the school library via telephone or mail.

Thirty credits are required for the MA degree; the MBA requires 57. Credits may be transferred from other schools and applied toward either degree. Upon completion of either degree, distance students are invited to attend commencement ceremonies on campus.

Regis University

External MBA
7600 East Orchard Road, Suite 100N
Englewood, CO 80111-2516

Degree awarded:	MBA
Areas of concentration:	General business
Admissions requirements:	Bachelor's degree, 2 years work experience, letters of recommendation, GMAT or 2 essays, faculty interview, resume
Media:	Internet, video, text, audio, CD-ROM
Total units in program:	30
Residency:	None
Accreditation:	Regional
Year founded:	1877
Ownership:	Nonprofit, private
Phone:	(800) 404-7355
Fax:	(303) 694-1554
E-mail:	mba@mbaregis.edu
Web site:	www.mbaregis.com

Applicants to Regis's external MBA program must have a Bachelor's degree, two years of significant full-time work experience, two letters of recommendation, and a current resume. They may either supply GMAT scores or write two essays from a list of six topics. Qualified applicants will be interviewed by Regis faculty over the telephone prior to starting the program.

The External MBA program is designed to meet the needs of working adults who do not live in Colorado or who are unable to attend on-site classes. Students participate in the 10-course, 30-credit-hour program through various forms of distance-learning technology. For each class, students are shipped textbooks, a study guide, and audio and video tapes, and participate in class discussions through e-mail and Internet bulletin boards. All classes are offered in an accelerated 8-week format, which gives students the flexibility of six start dates per year.

Each student is assigned an academic advisor for the duration of the program. This person serves as a resource for ongoing questions and degree completion advice. This is a tracked program, but all the classes are offered all the time, so students may take a term off and resume immediately without difficulty.

Rensselaer Polytechnic Institute

Lally School of Management and Technology
Professional and Distance Education (PDE)
C11 4011
Troy, NY 12180

Degree awarded:	MBA
Area of concentration:	General business
Admissions requirements:	Bachelor's degree, GMAT, essay, work experience, supervisor's approval
Media:	Television, videotapes, videoconferencing, World Wide Web
Total units in program:	30 credit hours
Residency:	None
Accreditation:	Regional, AACSB
Year founded:	1824
Ownership:	Nonprofit, independent
Phone:	(518) 276-7787
Fax:	(518) 276-8026
E-mail:	katchc@rpi.edu
Web site:	lallyschool.rpi.edu

Rensselaer's Professional and Distance Education (PDE) department works with corporate partners to bring distance-learning courses to the workplace. PDE currently serves 900 working professionals each semester from major international corporations, including Allied Signal, AT&T, DuPont, Ford, General Motors, IBM, Lockheed Martin, and Xerox.

The school's MBA program goes out to corporations around the globe via television programming, videoconferencing, prerecorded classes, and the World Wide Web. Students and professors interact in person or via videoconferencing, post, telephone, fax, e-mail, or the World Wide Web.

To be admitted to the program, applicants must hold a Bachelor's degree, submit GMAT scores, write an essay of intent, and have satisfactory work experience. They must also obtain corporate permission to participate in the program (i.e., the company must register as a corporate partner with Rensselaer). Distance learners enjoy the benefits of Rensselaer's school library, campus computer network, advising services, and e-mail. Credits may be transferred from other schools and applied toward the MBA.

Rensselaer's video network is also used to provide "live" office hours for off-campus students. Periodically, the faculty conducts interactive review sessions allowing students to call in with questions or comments. These broadcasts are also recorded on videotape at the site and are made available to students whose schedules do not permit real-time participation.

Saint Joseph's College

Department 840
278 Whites Bridge Road
Standish, ME 04084-5263

Degree awarded:	Master of Health Services Administration
Area of concentration:	Health services administration
Admissions requirements:	Bachelor's degree, letters of recommendation, essay of intent
Media:	Internet, e-mail, telephone, written assignments
Total units in program:	42
Residency:	Some
Accreditation:	Regional
Year founded:	1912
Ownership:	Church
Phone:	(207) 892-7841 • (800) 752-4723
Fax:	(207) 892-7480
E-mail:	pselbst@sjcme.edu
Web site:	www.sjcme.edu

A Master's in Health Services Administration is available as a distance degree. Admission requirements include a Bachelor's degree, letters of recommendation, and an essay of intent.

Forty-two of the required 48 semester hours must be completed at Saint Joseph's, and the school allows students 10 years to complete the program. Coursework is done as traditional written or e-mailed assignments. Some courses are available via the World Wide Web. Students may communicate with their teachers via e-mail, telephone and fax.

Two two-week residencies are required for degree completion.

Saint Leo University

3000 Northwest 83rd St.
Building R, Room 227
Gainesville, FL 32606

Degree awarded:	MBA
Area of concentration:	General business
Admissions requirements:	Bachelor's degree, transcripts, GMAT
Media:	Weekend classes
Total units in program:	12 courses
Residency:	Yes
Accreditation:	Regional
Year founded:	1890
Ownership:	Church
Phone:	(352) 588-8311
Fax:	(352) 395-5811
E-mail:	susan.steiner@saintleo.edu
Web site:	www.saintleo.edu

Saint Leo University has campuses at military bases and community colleges throughout Florida, as well as in Texas, Georgia, South Carolina, and Virginia. This network supports the school's MBA program, which meets three semesters per year on alternate Saturdays or Sundays. Through this program, all 12 required courses for the MBA are completed in 24 months.

Salve Regina University

Extension Study
100 Ochre Point Avenue
Newport, RI 02840-4192

Degrees offered:	MBA, MS in management, business administration, human development, and international relations
Areas of concentration:	General business, international relations, human development, management
Admissions requirements:	Bachelor's degree, GRE, MAT, or GMAT, 2 letters of recommendation
Media:	Mailed texts, e-mail, telephone, fax, Internet
Total units in program:	36
Residency:	Brief
Accreditation:	Regional
Year founded:	1934
Ownership:	Nonprofit, private
Phone:	(401) 847-6650, ext. 2229 • (800) 637-0002
Fax:	(401) 849-0702
E-mail:	Mistol@salve.edu
Web site:	www.salve.edu

Master's degrees in management, business administration, human development and international relations are offered through Salve Regina. These programs require 36 units to complete. An average of 6 credits are transferable toward this total from other institutions or per ACE guidelines. Exceptions are made for graduates of military colleges, who may transfer up to 18 credits. Students having completed CPCU's or ARM's courses also have the option to transfer up to 12 units toward the MBA or management degrees.

In all programs, instruction is by correspondence and guided independent study, supported by regular mail, e-mail, web-based courses and telephone contact with faculty. All programs require a brief residence of four days in the summer.

To be considered for the program, applicants must have a Bachelor's degree, either GRE, GMAT, or MAT scores, and two letters of recommendation, neither from a relative.

Southern Cross University

P.O. Box 157
Lismore NSW
Australia

Degree awarded:	MBA
Areas of concentration:	Finance, marketing, international business, small business and entrepreneurship, human resource management, sports management, health services management, tourism
Admission requirements:	Bachelor's degree, one year of work experience. Students whose first language is not English must provide proof of English-language proficiency (TOEFL 550, IELTS 6.0).
Media:	Printed study guides and books of readings; audiotapes and computer disks in some units.
Total units:	12 course units
Residency:	Optional
Accreditation:	GAAP
Year founded:	1970
Ownership:	State
Phone:	(61-2) 6620-3434
Fax:	(61-2) 6621-3876
E-mail:	intoff@scu.edu.au
Web site:	www.scu.edu.au/schools/gcm/mba

The Southern Cross MBA is available by distance learning in various cities in the countries of Australia, Hong Kong, Singapore, and New Zealand, and at individual centers in the cities of Shanghai, Port Moresby, and Kuala Lumpur. Instruction is by the same faculty who conduct the on-campus courses, with support from local tutors in overseas locations. Study materials, assessment, and other requirements are consistent across all locations. Each of the 12 courses comprises 1 unit, and takes an average of 150 study hours to complete. The program is offered on a trimester basis, with intakes in January, May, and September. A broad range of elective units can be undertaken in addition to the core management units. Course materials and assignments are workplace-focused and emphasize practical applications.

Southwest Missouri State University

Master of Science in CIS Program
CIS Dept., 359 Glass Hall
901 South National Ave.
Springfield, MO 65804

Degree awarded:	MS in computer information systems
Area of concentration:	Computer information systems
Admissions requirements:	Bachelor's degree, business courses, computer courses
Media:	Internet, traditional texts
Total units in program:	36 credit hours
Residency:	One week per semester
Accreditation:	Regional, AACSB
Year founded:	1905
Ownership:	Nonprofit, state
Phone:	(417) 836-4131
Fax:	(417) 836-6907
E-mail:	mscis@mail.smsu.edu
Web site:	www.mscis.smsu.edu

Southwest Missouri State's Master of Science in Computer Information Systems (MSCIS) is a four-semester program completed mostly over the Internet. By using e-mail, the World Wide Web, traditional texts, and a one-week residency at the beginning of each semester, distance students complete the 36 credit hours required of the program. Topics for the individual 3-credit courses include project management, end-user computing, resource acquisition, and database administration. Two of three offered electives (system development programming operations, operating systems, and special topics in IS) must be completed.

To qualify for the program, applicants must have three years of documented professional information systems work experience, a Bachelor's degree with a GPA of 2.75 or higher for the last 60 hours of credit, and an acceptable score on the GMAT. The prospective student must have taken at least 9 hours of information systems coursework from an institution of higher learning, including at least one course in each of the following areas: systems analysis and design, programming (any language), and database design and/or implementation. A background in business administration including exposure to accounting, finance, marketing, management and economics is also required. These business requirements may be satisfied by an undergraduate or graduate degree in business administration, or courses equivalent to at least a total of 9 hours from any three of the following business subjects: accounting, finance, marketing, management and/or economics.

Following each on-campus session, the learning continues off-campus using distance-learning technologies. Instruction includes case analysis, self-paced programs and on-line discussions using the Internet and e-mail. Students access course assignments and carry on discussions with professors and classmates from around the world.

Stephens College

School of Continuing Education
Campus Box 2083
Columbia, MO 65215

Degree Awarded:	MBA
Areas of concentration:	Management, entrepreneurship, information systems
Admissions requirements:	Internet access, GMAT, Bachelor's degree, 3.0 GPA
Media:	Internet, traditional texts
Total units in program:	51 credit hours
Residency:	Some
Accreditation:	Regional, AACSB
Year founded:	1833
Ownership:	Nonprofit, independent
Phone:	(573) 876-7125 • (800) 388-7579
Fax:	(573) 876-7248
E-mail:	grad@wc.stephens.edu
Web site:	www.stephens.edu

The Internet-based MBA Program is available to students worldwide. Students from around the globe connect with each other and Stephens College faculty members in discussions about business issues, case studies and assignments. Students may choose an emphasis in management, entrepreneurial studies or clinical information systems management.

During the program, students will visit the campus twice—once for a weekend orientation workshop during the first year and later for one week during the final capstone course. Three 10-week sessions will be offered throughout the year, during which students can enroll in a maximum of two courses per session.

MBA students are required to have access to e-mail and the Internet. To be admitted into the MBA program, a prospective student must complete the Graduate Management Admission Test (GMAT). The candidate's performance on the GMAT, combined with the undergraduate grade point average, are given primary consideration in the acceptance decision. A minimum GPA of 3.0 in the last 60 hours of undergraduate work is required. Students who have not completed the GMAT may enroll in a maximum of two courses on a conditional basis. They must complete the GMAT within six months of application, in addition to meeting the criteria for full admission.

Eight foundation courses (24 credit hours) at the undergraduate level are designed to provide a background for students who must fulfill undergraduate course requirements. Students who have successfully completed appropriate undergraduate coursework may be exempt from foundation courses. Nine graduate core courses (27 credit hours) provide a common body of knowledge for all students in the program.

Strayer University

Strayer Online
8382-F Terminal Road
Lorton, VA 22079

Degree awarded:	MBA
Area of concentration:	General business
Admissions requirements:	Bachelor's degree, GMAT or GRE, GPA of 2.75 or higher
Media:	Audioconferencing, World Wide Web, e-mail
Total units in program:	54 quarter-hour credits
Residency:	None
Accreditation:	Regional
Year founded:	1892
Ownership:	Proprietary
Phone:	(703) 339-1850
Fax:	(703) 339-1852
E-mail:	jet@strayer.edu
Web site:	www.strayer.edu

Strayer Online offers distance learning to qualified students via audioconferencing and the Internet. Entrance requirements for the distance MBA program are the same as expected of traditional students: a Bachelor's degree, GMAT or GRE scores, and a GPA of 2.75 or higher. Distance students must also have regular access to the World Wide Web. The distance curriculum is the same as that on campus, with distance students logging on to the Internet to check assignments and discuss the work with professors and fellow students.

During the scheduled class period, each class member accesses the University's computer system and participates on-line in a conversational mode with the instructor and other class members. In this mode, the student is assigned case studies, discussion questions, and problems. Students discuss the status of their term papers, articles, projects, and exams using the Internet. Attendance is recorded through e-mail, and written assignments are submitted via e-mail and fax.

Students can contact their instructors outside the scheduled Internet sessions by e-mail or phone. Exams are taken either at one of the campus locations or with local proctors.

Students taking classes through Strayer Online have the same admissions and financial aid requirements, policies and procedures, and student services and activities as those students taking classes in the traditional classroom environment.

Syracuse University

Independent Study Degree Programs
Syracuse, NY 13244-6020

Degree awarded:	MBA
Area of concentration:	General management
Admissions requirements:	Bachelor's degree, GMAT, essays, letters of recommendation
Media:	Traditional texts, e-mail, fax, Internet
Total units in program:	54
Residency:	Three weeklong stays per year
Accreditation:	Regional, AACSB
Year founded:	1870
Ownership:	Nonprofit, private
Phone:	(315) 443-9214
Fax:	(315) 443-9517
E-mail:	MBAinfo@som.syr.edu
Web site:	www.som.syr.edu

The Independent Study MBA through Syracuse University requires three seven-day residencies per year. Average MBA degree completion time is three to four years. Students are required to be on the Syracuse campus or at an optional off-campus residence site (London, Shanghai, etc.) for a week at the beginning of each trimester for a series of classes associated with each course offered in the program. These weeklong residence periods occur three times a year: in January, May, and August. Students then devote the remainder of the trimester to home study, conferring with their professors by telephone, fax, mail, and e-mail. Some classes involve team projects during the residencies and/or during the home study period. The Independent Study MBA emphasizes a broad, strategic management view of business. The curriculum consists of 54 credits of coursework, 39 of which are the program's core, focusing on the functional areas of management, law and public policy, organizational behavior, and economic theory, as well as on the tools of quantitative analysis. The remaining 15 credits of electives are drawn from the areas of accounting, finance, marketing, and organization and management.

The program enrolls students from most states and many foreign countries, who represent numerous prominent corporations and influential government agencies. When these students gather at the residencies, they take exams, attend lectures, do research, and renew relationships with professors and with each other.

Professional accreditation is from the International Association for Management Education (AACSB).

Texas A & M University

[handwritten: Eliminated program classes → http://tamu-commerce.edu /mba]

A&M Commerce
Graduate Admission Officer
The Graduate School
P O Box 3011
Commerce, TX 75429-3011

Degree awarded:	MBA
Area of concentration:	General business
Admissions requirements:	Bachelor's degree, 2.875 GPA or higher, 375 GMAT or higher
Media:	Internet
Total units in program:	10 courses (30 semester hours)
Residency:	None, although some proctored tests may be required
Accreditation:	Regional, AACSB
Year founded:	1889
Ownership:	Nonprofit, state
Phone:	(903) 886-5190
Fax:	N/A
E-mail:	MBA@tamu-commerce.edu
Web site:	http://mbaonline.tamu-commerce.edu

Distance students complete the MBA degree from Texas A&M by taking 10 courses (or thirty semester hours of coursework) online. The program allows students to complete assignments and communicate with professors and other students without any visits to campus, although some tests may require travel to a nearby testing facility.

A Bachelor's degree and above-average scores in GPA and the GMAT are required for admission to the program. The first five courses cover general business and finance, with in-depth management work and electives following.

Student services available to distance learners include access to the campus bookstore (students may order books via phone or email), career services, financial aid, and library resources.

Those interested in the MBA can apply online at the school's web site. Specific questions regarding the MBA program or courses may be directed toward Dr. Robert Seay, Director, at (903) 886-5190.

Thomas Edison State College

101 West State St
Trenton, NJ 08608-1176

Degree awarded:	MS in management
Area of concentration:	Management
Admissions requirements:	Bachelor's degree, five years of experience, computer skills
Media:	Internet
Total units in program:	36
Residency:	Two weekend sessions
Accreditation:	Regional
Year founded:	1972
Ownership:	Nonprofit, state
Phone:	(609) 984-1150
Fax:	(609) 984-8447
E-mail:	info@tesc.edu
Web site:	www.tesc.edu

The Master of Science in management degree serves employed adults who have had professional experience in the management field. The program integrates the theory and practice of management as it applies to diverse organizations, educational institutions, and other nonprofit agencies. The emphasis is on theory and practice in the management of organizations.

Students are required to attend two weekend residencies—an orientation at the beginning of the program, and a final session at the end. The location of each residency may be in New Jersey or in a city central to the students admitted into the program. Students are responsible for travel and lodging expenses.

Students may transfer in no more than 6 semester hours of graduate credits completed elsewhere. Thirty of the 36 credits required must be completed through Thomas Edison's independent computer-based graduate course offerings. Students communicate with their professors and classmates via the on-line computer classroom, as well as by e-mail.

A Bachelor's degree (in any field), at least five years of relevant work experience, fluency in written and presentation skills, and computer and management skills are all requisites for acceptance to the program.

Each student is expected to have a corporate/organizational mentor. In most cases this mentor is a person associated with the employment work site. This mentor is expected to help the student identify worksite issues to be integrated into the course of study.

Touro University International

10542 Calle Lee Suite 102
Los Alamitos, CA 90720

Degree awarded:	MBA
Areas of concentration:	General business, e-commerce, international business, health care management, information technology management
Admissions requirements:	Bachelor's degree, 3.0 GPA
Media:	Internet, CD-ROM
Total units in program:	32 semester credits
Residency:	None
Accreditation:	Regional
Year founded:	1970
Ownership:	Independent, nonprofit
Phone:	(714) 816-0366
Fax:	(714) 816-0367
E-mail:	info@tourou.edu
Web site:	www.tourouniversity.edu

Touro University International accepts up to 6 semester credits of Master level courses from accredited graduate-level institutions. Applicants without an undergraduate degree in business will be required to take one or more business courses to qualify for the MBA program.

The MBA requires students complete 6 required courses (for a total of 24 semester credits) and 2 elective courses (for 8 semester credits). Full-load students can expect to complete the program in as little as 15 months. A general business MBA can be completed, or students can specialize in one of the areas of e-commerce, international business, health care management, or information technology management, by choosing their elective courses in one of these fields.

Four sessions are held by Touro each year, each session lasting 12 weeks. Students register online and receive a CD-ROM for each course they take. The software complements the bulk of the learning which is done online. Touro's "cyber classroom" allows students and professors to interact via audio and visual technologies online. No thesis is required for the degree.

Touro provides academic advising to distance students via e-mail, post, or telephone. Tech support is provided by the university, and an online library is available for student reference.

Université de Moncton

Education Permanente
Moncton, NB E1A 3E9
Canada

Degree awarded:	MBA
Area of concentration:	General business
Admissions requirements:	Bachelor's degree, letter of recommendation, work experience
Media:	Videoconferencing, World Wide Web, and e-mail
Total units in program:	45 credits
Residency:	None
Accreditation:	GAAP
Year founded:	1963
Ownership:	Nonprofit, state
Phone:	(506) 858-4121
Fax:	(506) 858-4489
E-mail:	blancha@umoncton.ca
Web site:	www.umoncton.ca/educ-perm/eduperm.html

Six off-campus centers in Bathurst, Campbellton, Edmundston, La Butte, Moncton, and Shippagan are equipped to deliver courses to distance MBA students, or students can have the coursework delivered to them at home. Classes are taken using videoconferencing, e-mail, and the World Wide Web, and distance students may be required to have an Internet-ready computer. The program is limited to Canadian students, and if you don't speak French, the Web site won't do you a lot of good.

Distance learners must complete 45 credits to earn their MBA degree. Aside from the coursework, credits may be earned through examinations, portfolio assessment, or through transfers from other schools. Five years are allowed for completion of the program.

University of Colorado-Colorado Springs

Graduate School of Business
1420 Auston Bluffs Parkway
Colorado Springs, CO 80933

Degree awarded:	MBA
Area of concentration:	General business
Admissions requirements:	Bachelor's degree, GMAT, computer, TV and VCR
Media:	Internet, television, video
Total units in program:	36–51 credit hours
Residency:	None
Accreditation:	Regional, AACSB
Year founded:	1965
Ownership:	Nonprofit, state
Phone:	(719) 262-3408 • (800) 777-MIND
Fax:	(719) 262-3100
E-mail:	ksangerm@mail.uccs.edu
Web site:	www.uccs.edu/~collbus/new/jecmain.htm

The University of Colorado at Colorado Springs offers an MBA via distance learning in cooperation with Jones Knowledge Group. This program uses a number of technologies, including video, cable and the Internet. The majority of the coursework and student/faculty interaction is delivered via the Internet.

Courses for the program are delivered through a combination of video presentations, Internet-based materials and communication with classmates and professors. Up to 3 hours of coursework may be taken prior to admission. Successful completion of MBA coursework taken prior to the application process does not guarantee admission to the program. Application for admission should be made during the first semester of enrollment. Applicants are required to have a Bachelor's degree from a regionally accredited institution and must submit GMAT results, official transcripts, and a current resume. Students enrolled in the MBA will also need access to the following: a television with a VCR, a Pentium PC or comparable Mac, and a 28.8 KBPS or faster modem with access to the World Wide Web.

The MBA program requires 36 credit hours of coursework plus an additional 15 hours of foundation work, which may be waived based on a student's prior academic background. Six credit hours from an AACSB-accredited program may be transferred towards degree requirements. The MBA degree may be completed in as little as two years, even with a full-time career.

Candidates for the MBA degree are expected to complete the degree within a five-year period. Professional accreditation is from the International Association for Management Education (AACSB).

University of Dallas

Graduate School of Management
1845 East Northgate Drive
Irving, TX 75062-4799

Degrees awarded:	MBA, Master of Management
Area of concentration:	Health services management
Admissions requirements:	Bachelor's degree, any two of the following--GPA of 3.0 or better, high GMAT, 5 or more years of managerial or professional work experience
Media:	Internet, video
Total units in program:	16 courses/48 hours
Residency:	None
Accreditation:	Regional, AACSB
Year founded:	1956
Ownership:	Nonprofit, church
Phone:	(972) 385-7696 • (800) 832-5622
Fax:	(972) 721-5254
E-mail:	cfdl@gte.net
Web site:	www.udallas.edu

Dallas's MBA in health services management is available entirely by courses offered at health care worksites (hospitals and other facilities). Only employees of facilities receiving either the HSTN or the Westcott network over their cable service may enroll. The program takes two to three years. Students who already have an MBA earn the Master of Management instead.

The degree is earned by completing 16 courses, a total of 48 semester hours. Those students working toward the MBA will automatically be granted a certificate after completing five specialized Health Services courses. Strategy, finance, legalities, and insurance are covered in the core courses and electives. UD has developed partnerships with major telecommunications companies where corporate employees are able to take graduate level courses at their work location using video conferencing systems and the Internet. Students may take the certificate program alone, or use those courses together with core business courses to earn the MBA.

UD is eager to form new partnerships with companies in the telecommunications industry. Learn more about existing programs or about forming new partnerships by sending an e-mail to the Center for Distance Learning at the e-mail address above.

University of Durham

Business School
Mill Hill Lane
Durham City
DH1 3LB
United Kingdom

Degree awarded:	MBA
Area of concentration:	General business
Admissions requirements:	Bachelor's degree and management experience
Media:	Texts, written materials, audiocassettes
Total units in program:	Four stages: stages 1 through 3 each consist of 4 subjects; stage 4 is by dissertation
Residency:	Some
Accreditation:	Regional
Year founded:	1832
Ownership:	Nonprofit, state
Phone:	(44-191) 374-2216
Fax:	(44-191) 374-3389
E-mail:	mbadl.enq@durham.ac.uk
Web site:	www.dur.ac.uk/dubs/dlmba.htm

In mid-1988 Durham introduced a Distance-Learning MBA (they have offered a traditional MBA since 1967). The program is administered by the University Business School to students in more than forty countries. The three- to four-year course of study is delivered through specially written distance-learning materials, annotated texts, and audiocassettes. One-week intensive residential seminars (first year excluded) are also available. It is one of only a handful of distance learning programmes accredited by the Association of MBAs, the UK accrediting body.

The MBA is taught in four stages. Stage one covers the basics: organizational behavior, marketing principles, accounting fundamentals, and quantitative topics. Stage two prepares students for human resources and financial management, strategic marketing, and information systems. Stage three, involving core studies business policy and operations management and two electives, may be combined with stage four, a dissertation. Examinations are offered at the school and at more than sixty outposts around the globe.

There are two alternative entry routes. Students entering directly into the MBA program must have a minimum of two years relevant work experience and hold a first degree or an approved equivalent professional qualification. An Advanced Diploma in Business Administration, which comprises the first two stages of the MBA, is offered with possible transfer to the MBA program after passing Stage 1 examinations. This requires considerable management experience, typically 3 years minimum, with a minimum age of 25.

University of Florida

Warrington College of Business Administration
PO Box 117152
134 Bryan Hall
Gainesville, FL 32611-7152

Degree awarded:	MBA
Area of concentration:	General business
Admissions requirements:	Bachelor's degree, GMAT, essay, letter of recommendation, work experience, and interview
Media:	Video- and audioconferencing, traditional texts, Internet, and computer software
Total units in program:	48 semester credits
Residency:	Three-day weekends on campus at the end of each term
Accreditation:	Regional, AACSB
Year founded:	1853
Ownership:	Nonprofit, state
Phone:	(352) 392-7992
Fax:	(352) 392-8791
E-mail:	treale@notes.cba.ufl.edu
Web site:	www.cba.ufl.edu/mba

Students in the University of Florida's distance MBA program are taught through a wide array of media, including video- and audioconferencing, CD-ROM and floppy disk computer software, World Wide Web, e-mail, computer conferencing, and traditional texts. Interaction with fellow students and professors can be done by virtually any of these means, and is also welcomed via telephone and fax. Because of the variety of media, students are required to have a laptop computer with 2 GB of hard drive space, an 8x CD-ROM drive, Windows 95, Office 97, and Internet connectivity. A camera is also required for some of the coursework.

Students are accepted from around the world, and each must possess a Bachelor's degree and GMAT scores, and must submit an essay of intent, one or more letters of recommendation, and proof of sufficient work experience. Applicants are also subject to an interview.

Three-day residency sessions are held on-campus at the culmination of each of four terms, and it is during these times that students take final exams, make presentations on their work, and meet the faculty they will be working with during the coming term. In addition to the 48 semester credits, a one-week European trip is completed.

Students are allowed twenty months to complete the coursework necessary for their degree. Distance learners have access to the University's library, advisors, computer system, e-mail, and career placement services.

University of Guelph

Room 221, MacLachlan Building
Guelph, ON N1G 2W1
Canada

Degree awarded:	MBA
Area of concentration:	Agriculture
Admissions requirements:	Bachelor's degree, essay of intent, letter of recommendation, work experience, resume
Media:	Computer software, Lotus Notes
Total units in program:	11 courses
Residency:	Seven-day summer session
Accreditation:	Regional
Year founded:	1964
Ownership:	Nonprofit, state
Phone:	(888) MBA-AGRI
Fax:	(519) 767-1510
E-mail:	mbaagri@uoguelph.ca
Web site:	www.mbaagri.uoguelph.ca

The University of Guelph offers a computer-based MBA in agriculture in conjunction with Athabasca University. Students interact and discuss assignments using Lotus Notes. It is required of all students that they have a Pentium processor computer with CD-ROM, 16 MB of RAM, 1 GB of hard drive space, and either Windows 95 or NT as an operating system. The school provides MS Office and Lotus Notes.

To enroll in the program, students need an undergraduate degree and/or substantive experience in operating a commercial farm or business, or managing within an organization. Students should be willing to devote 20–25 hours a week to the program and be prepared to spend a week in residence at the University of Guelph between core management and intensive agribusiness courses.

The MBA is divided into three distinct phases. Upon successful completion of the comprehensive examination and phase one, the student is rewarded with an Advanced Graduate Diploma in Management. Phase two consists of courses designed to provide students with skills and concepts specific to agribusiness. Finally, for phase three, the student is expected to complete a dissertation. Upon successful completion of all three phases (usually taking between 2 to 3 years), the student will receive the MBA.

University of Leicester

North American Representative:
Financial Times Management, Inc.
Two World Trade Center, Suite 1700
New York, NY 10048

Degree awarded:	MS in training
Areas of concentration:	Training, human resource management
Admissions requirements:	Bachelor's degree or academic credential plus 3 years work experience
Media:	Readings and papers
Total units in program:	36 credit hours
Residency:	None
Accreditation:	GAAP
Year founded:	1921
Ownership:	Nonprofit, public
Phone:	(212) 390-5030 • (888) 534-2378
Fax:	(212) 344-3469
E-mail:	
Web site:	www.ftknowledge.com

Leicester offers a Master of Science in training entirely by distance learning. To earn the degree, students do extensive reading in each of four five-month modules, writing a paper at the end of each module. Help is available by telephone, fax, e-mail, and an optional residential weekend each year. An interactive web board is being developed on-line.

There are no examinations; grading is instead based on the four papers, plus a final thesis. Students who put in ten hours a week on the program complete the degree in two years. The degree is designed not only for experienced trainers and human resource managers, but also for people interested in entering those fields.

Applicants should have either a Bachelor's degree or an academic credential plus three years of related experience. Those without a Bachelor's degree can enter the Master's program by successfully completing one of Leicester's one-year diploma programs.

University of Leicester

University Road
Leicester, LE1 7RH
United Kingdom

Degree awarded:	MBA
Areas of concentration:	General business, finance, marketing, educational management
Admissions requirements:	Bachelor's degree, references, work experience
Media:	Text-based
Total units in program:	15 units, 2 electives, final project
Residency:	None
Accreditation:	GAAP
Year founded:	1921
Ownership:	State
Phone:	(44-116) 252-5520
Fax:	(44-116) 252-3949
E-mail:	lumc@le.ac.uk
Web site:	www.le.ac.uk/lumc

Leicester offers a number of distance-learning Master's degrees to students world-wide from its headquarters in Britain or through other agents. An MBA is offered for students in the Far and Middle East. Study centers for students in this program have been established in Hong Kong, Singapore, Malaysia, Thailand, Indonesia, Japan, Taiwan, Dubai, Oman, and Saudi Arabia. There is also an MBA with a concentration in educational management for qualified teachers.

The MBA program covers a wide range of issues and aims to increase a manager's ability to make good strategic decisions. The MBA can be studied via flexible learning, with optional concentrations available in finance, marketing, total quality management, employment relations, and maritime management.

Students are introduced to the concepts of strategic management, including legal constraints on management, processes of organizational policy making, and management by objectives. Some of the topics covered include corporate growth, mergers and takeovers, competition policy, decision making, marketing strategy, and research and development (products and process).

The program is assessed 50% by continuous assessment, 50% by examination. Unsatisfactory assignments may be resubmitted once and exams may be retaken once.

University of London

Royal Holloway College
Room 1w
Senate House, Malet Street
London WC1E 7HU
United Kingdom.

Degree awarded:	MBA
Areas of concentration:	Management, several global and international concentrations
Admissions requirements:	Bachelor's degree, GMAT, 3 years work experience
Media:	Traditional texts
Total units in program:	6 required courses, 2 electives
Residency:	None
Accreditation:	GAAP
Year founded:	1836
Ownership:	Nonprofit, state
Phone:	+44 (0)171 862 8360
Fax:	+44 (0)171 862 8358
E-mail:	enquiries@external.lon.ac.uk
Web site:	www.lon.ac.uk/external/mba/mba.htm

The University of London's MBA prepares graduates for a career in international business. The school requires that students complete the program in no fewer than 28 months, although five years are allowed. The 28-month plan can be completed through a 20-hour per week study commitment.

Students receive a study package for each course they enroll in, which includes all the reading material for the course. Assignments are mailed to the University and exams are given in May or June at exam centers worldwide.

Topics covered in the MBA's six core courses are accounting and finance, marketing, human resources management and organizational behavior, operations management and information systems, business strategy, and business economics. These courses are designed to emphasize the University of London's commitment to preparing graduates for international business.

In addition to the required courses, students choose two electives from a list that includes multinational business practices, Asia Pacific business, global financial markets, and international business law. A business research report of 12,000 words is required at the end of the MBA program.

University of Maryland

University College
University Blvd at Adelphi Road
College Park, MD 20742

Degrees awarded:	MBA, MS in management, Master of International Management
Areas of concentration:	General business, management
Admissions requirements:	Bachelor's degree, essay
Media:	Written assignments over the Internet
Total units in program:	36–39, 42 for MBA
Residency:	None
Accreditation:	Regional, AACSB
Year founded:	1947
Ownership:	Nonprofit, state
Phone:	(301) 985-7000 • (800) 888-UMUC
Fax:	(301) 985-4611
E-mail:	gradschool@info.umuc.edu
Web site:	www.umuc.edu

The University of Maryland offers a wholly online MBA to be completed within 24 months. Students are grouped in cohorts, and each cohort is assigned to an individual faculty member. Six key themes are covered in the program: global challenges, systems thinking, problem solving, ethics and social responsibility, the impact of technology on management, and the future of organizations. Two orientation courses (also wholly online) must be completed before the student is eligible to enroll in the MBA program.

The Master of Science in management program focuses on theories and skills needed to lead and manage public, private, and nonprofit organizations. The program is designed for professionals who, as they assume increasing responsibility within their organizations, recognize the importance of expertise in a particular area with breadth of knowledge across key organizational processes. The degree program consists of six 3-credit core courses, five 3-credit track courses, and one 3-credit management project (two courses can be done in lieu of the project).

The Master of International Management (MIM) is a program for midcareer professionals pursuing careers in international business and commerce. It is designed to fill what the school sees as a void in traditional business education. It prepares students to deal with an increasing number of issues surrounding international business, including cultural differences, fluctuating exchange rates, trade regulations, foreign competition, and the opening of world markets.

Applicants need to have a Bachelor's degree and fill out the school's application form, which includes an essay on goals and intentions. Coursework is done over the Internet, with students logging in, downloading assignments, and writing replies. Tests are also administered on-line. No residency is required.

University of Natal

Private Bag X10
Dalbridge 4014
South Africa

Degree awarded:	MBA
Area of concentration:	General business
Admissions requirements:	Bachelor's degree
Media:	Independent study
Total units in program:	
Residency:	In-person final evaluation
Accreditation:	GAAP
Year founded:	1910
Ownership:	Nonprofit, state
Phone:	(27-31) 260-1111
Fax:	(27-31) 260 2214
E-mail:	strong@admin.und.ac.za
Web site:	www.und.ac.za

The University of Natal offers its Master's degrees through both taught coursework and through a research-based course of study. In the latter path, there is no coursework; the degree candidate does individual, independent research, culminating in a thesis that is submitted for in-person examinations. The school has two semi-independent campuses, one at Dalbridge/Durban, the other at Pietermaritzburg.

MBA specializations are currently only offered through residential study, but within the next 2 years, Natal expects to offer them to distance students as well (for now, distance students can do only a general MBA, without specialization). Concentrations offered are as follows: strategic financial management, strategic human resource management, strategic marketing management, environmental management, international business management, and maritime transport economics and management.

University of Northumbria at Newcastle

Flexible Management Learning Centre
Newcastle Business School
Northumberland Building
Newcastle Upon Tyne, NE1 8ST
United Kingdom

Degree awarded:	MBA
Area of concentration:	General business
Admissions requirements:	See below
Media:	Internet-based discussion and writing
Total units in program:	180 credit points
Residency:	None
Accreditation:	GAAP
Year founded:	1969
Ownership:	Nonprofit, independent
Phone:	(44-191) 227-4942
Fax:	(44-191) 227-4684
E-mail:	d.thompson@unn.ac.uk
Web site:	fmlc.unn.ac.uk

Ten years ago, the Newcastle Business School established a performance-oriented flexible MBA for working managers and professionals that allowed them to study and develop largely at home and work, with limited attendance. With the advent of widespread Internet use, NBS now offers the program internationally. Distant participants follow the same core study program as those who live and work near the University, except that their communication and patterns of contact are different. Face-to-face meetings are replaced or complemented by individual and group e-mail discussions and on-line activities.

There are no mandatory specific qualifications for entry into the program. Because of the nature of the program and the time demands, which are estimated at 10–12 hours a week, participants must show that they have the opportunity at work to carry out the required learning activities, can manage the intellectual demands of the program, and have the energy and motivation to complete a demanding program over 2–3 years. It is generally better for the participant if his or her employer is fully supportive of the program.

Coursework involves integrating theoretical perspectives with personal experiences. Participants personalize their development with close reference to their job demands and organizational context. A series of learning projects are carried out in the main management areas of resources, people, information and activities, and further work is done in marketing, strategy, leadership, and leading change. Credits are accumulated, with 180 required for the awarding of the MBA.

University of Notre Dame

Executive Programs
126 College of Business Administration
Notre Dame, IN 46556

Degree awarded:	MBA
Area of concentration:	General business
Admissions requirements:	Bachelor's degree, 5+ years experience
Media:	Videoconferencing
Total units in program:	63 credit hours
Residency:	Must live near one of four remote locations
Accreditation:	Regional, AACSB
Year founded:	1842
Ownership:	Church
Phone:	(219) 631-5285 • (800) 631-3622
Fax:	(219) 631-6783
E-mail:	CBA.execprog.1@nd.edu
Web site:	www.nd.edu/~execprog

Notre Dame's Executive MBA program uses the same course material for distance students that it does for those in on-campus classrooms. Videoconferencing technology creates a "virtual classroom," linking participating executives from all over into one interactive class setting.

Programs may originate from either of the College of Business Administration's two distance-education classrooms. The classroom systems feature fully interactive 2-way audio, 2-way compressed video technology over a multipoint dial-up network or T-1 transmission lines, ensuring near broadcast-quality video in real time.

The Executive MBA Program has 4 remote classrooms that are currently video-conferencing with the classrooms at Notre Dame. Two sites are in Indianapolis, one in Toledo, Ohio, and the fourth in Hoffman Estates, Illinois. Because classes are not offered as correspondence courses or through the Internet, students will need to attend the classes at one of the remote sites.

The two-year, four-semester program prepares students to be effective leaders in the workplace. The curriculum includes emphasis in the area of the so-called "fourth branch of the government" (the regulatory agencies), and on social and ethical issues of concern to managers. Students are required to maintain a 3.0 cumulative grade point average to graduate.

Applicants are required to have a Bachelor's degree, GMAT scores and five or more years of management experience. Some refresher courses in mathematics and certain Microsoft applications are available for those who need them.

Professional accreditation is from the International Association for Management Education (AACSB).

University of Paisley

High Street
Paisley, PA1 2BE
Scotland

Degree awarded:	MBA
Areas of concentration:	Marketing, quality management, real estate management
Admissions requirements:	Bachelor's degree, 3+ years work experience
Media:	Internet and multimedia software applications
Total units in program:	9 courses, final project
Residency:	None
Accreditation:	GAAP
Year founded:	1897
Ownership:	Private
Phone:	(44-141) 848-3000
Fax:	(44-141) 887-0812
E-mail:	dlu@paisley.ac.uk
Web site:	www.paisley.ac.uk

MBAs with concentrations in marketing and total quality management are offered. Non-U.K. students also qualify for the MBA in Real Estate Management. All study materials are provided in printed and electronic form, and coursework is accomplished via written lessons, multimedia and the Internet.

A computer with Windows 95 and access to the World Wide Web is standard equipment for distance learning from Paisley. Through their computer, students access the school's "virtual campus," a subset of Paisley's web site, and pull assignments off it for review. "Virtual classrooms" are available for each program module, supporting peer-group discussion and tutor-led activities. Computer conferencing is also provided for "real time" discussion between tutors and student groups. Coursework is completed and returned via e-mail. A tutoring team is set up for the students in the course.

Students receive a number of study modules, prepared in a way that presents information in a clear, easy-to-learn style. They also incorporate many helpful features, such as regular self-assessment questions to enable students to check their progress, and practical exercises that relate learning to the workplace. All study modules are reviewed regularly to keep them up-to-date. They consist of various multimedia elements, including specific software when necessary. All general communications between students and tutors are carried out through the virtual campus.

Student handbooks are issued, providing study tips and information on staff support. Tutors are assigned to students and issue them regular assessments to gauge progress in the course. Feedback is given to students to help them proceed.

University of Phoenix Online

Online Program Administrative Offices
100 Spear Street
San Francisco, CA 94105

Degree awarded:	MBA
Areas of concentration:	General business, also features specializations in accounting, technology management, and global management
Admissions requirements:	Bachelor's degree, GPA of 2.5 or higher, 3+ years experience, access to the World Wide Web
Media:	Internet
Total units in program:	51 semester credits
Residency:	None
Accreditation:	Regional, AACSB
Year founded:	1976
Ownership:	Proprietary
Phone:	(800) 742-4742
Fax:	(415) 541-0761
E-mail:	online@apollo/uophx.edu
Web site:	www.uophx.edu/online2

In 1989, the Arizona-based University of Phoenix began offering degrees entirely via computer, through program headquarters in San Francisco. On-line students get their assignments, have group discussions, and ask questions of their professors over the Internet, without leaving their homes or offices. Each class meeting is spread out over an entire week, allowing busy students to complete their work at the most convenient time for them. Computer training and orientation is provided once a student enrolls.

The on-line program mirrors the University of Phoenix's correspondence program in all other aspects.

University of Phoenix

Center for Distance Education
4625 East Elwood Street
P.O. Box 52076
Phoenix, AZ 85072

Degree awarded:	MBA
Areas of concentration:	General business, also features specializations in health care management, technology management, and global management
Admissions requirements:	Bachelor's degree, GPA of 2.5 or higher, 3 years experience
Media:	Written correspondence
Total units in program:	51 semester credits
Residency:	None
Accreditation:	Regional, AACSB
Year founded:	1976
Ownership:	Proprietary
Phone:	(602) 921-8014 • (800) 366-9699
Fax:	(602) 894-2152
E-mail:	rrpaden@apollogrp.edu
Web site:	www.uophx.edu

In addition to the San Francisco-based on-line programs discussed in the prior entry, Phoenix also offers a text-based MBA with an optional concentration in technology management. Study takes place by correspondence, with support given via telephone, fax and mail.

One of the major program activities for the MBA degree is the successful completion of a managerial business plan. Called the Applied Management Science Project, this is an exercise in practical, professional management planning, involving the student's present workplace. Proficiency with spreadsheet software will help the student advance quickly.

Applicants must be employed or have verifiable access to a suitable work environment in which to complete classroom assignments. A Bachelor's degree, GPA of 2.5 or better, and three or more years of business-related experience are musts. Books may be purchased through a toll-free number and students have access to financial aid, a learning resource center, and free assessments of their progress.

To complete their degree, students must complete 51 semester credits (12 of which may come from an outside source). The satisfactory completion of the final test and the Applied Management Science Project are also necessary.

University of Pittsburgh

The Joseph M. Katz
Graduate School of Business
276 Mervis Hall
Pittsburgh, PA 15260

Degree awarded:	MBA
Area of concentration:	General business
Admissions requirements:	Bachelor's degree, GMAT, essay, letter of recommendation, work experience, calculus
Media:	Audiocassettes and computer software
Total units in program:	51 credits
Residency:	13 weeks total on campus
Accreditation:	Regional, AACSB
Year founded:	1787
Ownership:	Nonprofit, state
Phone:	(412) 648-1700
Fax:	(412) 648-1659
E-mail:	info@katz.business.pitt.edu
Web site:	www.pitt.edu/~business

First offered in 1991, the University of Pittsburgh's distance-education classes, taught through a variety of means, have helped executives earn their MBA. Audiocassettes, computer software, Internet programming, and traditional texts combine in this 51-credit program. Students interact with professors and each other through in-person meetings, telephone, fax, and the Internet. A computer is required of all students.

To enroll in the program, students must have a Bachelor's degree, GMAT scores, an essay of intent, one or more letters of recommendation, work experience, and a background in calculus. Credits may be transferred from other sources, and examinations may be arranged to earn credits. Distance learners have access to regular student facilities such as the computer network, library, and tutoring.

Two years are allowed for completion of the program, and distance students can expect to spend 13 weeks on campus (each residency is taken in 1–2 week blocks) over the duration of their studies.

University of Saint Francis

500 Wilcox Street
Joliet, IL 60435

Degrees awarded:	MBA, MS in Management, MS in Health Services Administration
Areas of concentration:	Management, health services
Admissions requirements:	Bachelor's degree, 2.75 GPA or higher, computer competency, two years of work experience, "verification of employment" form
Media:	Internet
Total units in program:	48 credit hours
Residency:	None
Accreditation:	
Year founded:	1920
Ownership:	Church
Phone:	(815) 740-3360 • (800) 735-4723
Fax:	(815) 740-3537
E-mail:	jthompson@stfrancis.edu
Web site:	www.stfrancis.edu/grdline/index_gp.htm

While St. Francis' MS in Management and MS in Continuing Education and Management require students to take a combination of online and residential classes, the MBA and MS in Health Services Administration degrees may be earned entirely online. MBA students may specialize in management or health services.

Foundation courses compose up to 12 hours of the 48 required for the degree, although students should check with their advisors to determine if any of the foundation courses may be waived due to previous experience. Up to eight credit hours may be waived in this fashion.

Prospective students should have a Bachelor's degree and a graduating GPA of 2.75 or higher. Computer competency and business employment are verified before entering the program. The MBA program takes two years to complete. A one-year program is available, but only for students who combine residential and online learning.

All learning is done via Internet. Discussions and assignments are handled through specialized web pages. St. Francis' web site has an online "help desk" to troubleshoot common problems. Distance students have access to academic advising via e-mail and telephone, and the bookstore and library via the Web.

University of Saint Thomas

Graduate School of Business
1000 LaSalle Avenue
MPL 100
Minneapolis, MN 55403

Degree awarded:	MBA
Area of concentration:	Medical group management
Admissions requirements:	Bachelor's degree, GMAT, essay, letter of recommendation, resume, two years work experience
Media:	Internet, traditional texts, computer software
Total units in program:	50 semester credits
Residency:	Two one-week sessions every year
Accreditation:	Regional, AACSB
Year founded:	1885
Ownership:	Church
Phone:	(651) 462-4135 • (800) 328-6819
Fax:	(651) 962-4410
E-mail:	shagel@stthomas.edu
Web site:	www.stthomas.edu

Saint Thomas's MBA program in medical group management covers all of the basic concepts and prerequisites found in standard MBA programs, and then applies those concepts to the health care profession and, more specifically, to the medical group environment. The program also includes many specialized courses designed to provide the technical knowledge required to effectively manage medical groups.

The majority of the instruction occurs over the Internet, with two one-week sessions on campus each year, for the duration of the program. The school uses the diversity of its students and faculty, who live in all parts of the United States, to address the national aspects of health care business education.

A Bachelor's degree and GMAT scores, as well as an essay of intent, one or more letters of recommendation, and two or more years of work experience are all necessary for applicants to the program. Completion of the MBA takes between two and three years.

University of San Francisco

McLaren School of Business
2130 Fulton Street
San Francisco, CA 94117-1045

Degree awarded:	MBA
Areas of concentration:	Finance, international business, management, marketing, and telecommunications management and policy programs
Admissions requirements:	Bachelor's degree, GMAT, essay, work experience
Media:	Internet, video- and audiocassettes, traditional texts
Total units in program:	48 semester units
Residency:	Some
Accreditation:	Regional, AACSB
Year founded:	1855
Ownership:	Church
Phone:	(415) 422-6771
Fax:	(415) 422-2502
E-mail:	McLaren@usfca.edu
Web site:	www.usfca.edu/mclaren

In conjunction with corporate partners, the University of San Francisco offers an MBA through a variety of methods, mostly Internet based. Distance students must be employees of participating corporations in order to have access to the program, and tuition is paid for by the employer. The university would like us to emphasize that no students are admitted unless they are employees of a corporate partner.

Five areas of emphasis are offered as concentrations in the MBA program: finance, international business, management, marketing, and telecommunications management and policy programs. Each specialization is tailored to place graduates in executive-level positions relevant to their studies.

Aside from corporate membership, prospective students must possess a Bachelor's degree, GMAT scores, and two or more years of work experience to qualify for the program. Forty-eight semester units are completed within two years, and certain capstone courses require residencies in San Francisco.

Distance students have access to the school's computer network and advising services. In addition, programs are held at the school to aid in job placement, and may be attended during the residencies.

University of Sarasota

5250 17th Street
Sarasota, FL 34235

Degrees awarded:	MBA, Master of International Business
Areas of concentration:	Finance, marketing, human resources, health care administration, international trade
Admissions requirements:	Bachelor's degree, resume, and three references
Media:	Traditional on-campus work combined with correspondence tutorials
Total units in program:	36
Residency:	Some
Accreditation:	Regional
Year founded:	1969
Ownership:	Private, independent
Phone:	(941) 379-0404 • (800) 331-5995
Fax:	(941) 379-9464
E-mail:	univsar@compuserve.com
Web site:	www.sarasota.edu

Sarasota offers both a distance MBA and a short-residency Master of International Business (MIB). Admission to the MBA program is open to applicants holding a Bachelor's degree. The admission decision is based upon a grade point average of at least 3.0 on a 4.0 scale for work leading to the Bachelor's degree and any subsequent graduate study. A resume and three recommendations are also necessary. Up to 6 credits may be transferred toward the degree.

The distance MBA is taught through a combination of distance modules and brief residencies. Students proceed through the program as part of a study cohort. An emphasis can be chosen within one of five concentrations: finance, marketing, human resources, health care administration, and international trade.

The MIB is offered, in partnership with other universities in North America, to managers in the U.S., Canada, and Mexico. Its goal is to train managers in these countries to achieve the objectives set out by NAFTA. Students study in cohort groups and meet the residency requirements by attending four one-week sessions: one in Florida, one in Montreal, one in Puebla, Mexico, and the final one in California. Admission to this program is open to qualified applicants holding an accredited undergraduate degree from one of the three NAFTA countries. The admission decision is based on a GPA of 3.0 during the last two years of undergraduate study (and any subsequent graduate study), professional statement and three recommendations, TOEFL score of at least 500 for those for whom English is not a first language and, if deemed necessary, an interview with faculty.

University of Southern Queensland

Faculty of Business
Toowoomba
Queensland, 4350
Australia

Degree Awarded:	MBA
Areas of concentration:	Environmental management, human resource management, information systems, international business, marketing, project management, occupational health and safety, finance, accounting, law
Admissions requirements:	Bachelor's degree, five years business experience
Media:	Computer applications and printed study materials
Total units in program:	12 credit points
Residency:	Optional
Accreditation:	GAAP
Year founded:	1967
Ownership:	Nonprofit, state
Phone:	+61 (07) 4631 1881
Fax:	+61 (07) 4631 2811
E-mail:	bizness@usq.edu.au
Web site:	www.usq.edu.au

The MBA offered by Southern Queensland is for graduates from any discipline who have considerable business experience and a potential for managerial status at their corporation. Students learn the basics of business administration through developing judgment, skills, and attitudes. Concentrations available are: environmental management, human resource management, information systems, international business, marketing, project management, occupational health and safety, finance, accounting, and law.

Students learn through a combination of computer applications. Methods differ from unit to unit, but may include multimedia, videoconferencing, and the Internet.

The MBA consists of 12 credit points, 8 earned from core, or "foundation" classes, and 4 from electives, also known as "disciplines." Students will normally be required to complete the foundation management units before progressing to the other units.

Candidates for entry into the MBA must have a Bachelor's degree and five years of work experience. Students not meeting these entry criteria may be permitted to enroll in the Graduate Certificate in Management initially. Satisfactory performance will ensure entry into the Graduate Diploma in Management or directly into the MBA. Full credit towards the MBA will be granted for prior successful studies in the Graduate Certificate in Management and/or the Graduate Diploma in Management programs.

University of Stirling

Course Administrator
MBA in Retailing (ASEAN)
Institute for Retail Studies
Stirling, Scotland
FK9 4LA
United Kingdom

Degree awarded:	MBA
Areas of concentration:	Retailing and wholesaling
Admissions requirements:	Bachelor's degree
Media:	Texts, written coursework exchanged through the mail
Total units in program:	14 units
Residency:	Three weekends and one tutorial per year
Accreditation:	GAAP
Year founded:	1967
Ownership:	State
Phone:	(44-1786) 467-386
Fax:	(44-1786) 465-290
E-mail:	mba-retail@stir.ac.uk
Web site:	www.stir.ac.uk/marketing/irs/irsframe.htm

A distance MBA in retailing and wholesaling is offered by Scotland's University of Stirling. The program was founded over ten years ago in a cooperative effort between Stirling and British retail groups Tesco, Marks and Spencer, the Burton Group, W.H. Smith, the National Retail Training Council, and the Distributive Industries Training Trust.

The majority of the teaching in the program is done by Stirling faculty, in conjunction with other academics, retail practitioners, and other industry tutors. Students are supplied with written course material and all required textbooks and articles, and attend three residential weekends per year and one tutorial per unit.

The program involves each student completing fourteen units, which would typically be covered in a two-and-a-half year period. The fourteen units are divided into three categories. The first category comprises eight units covering topic areas such as people and finance management, research, and business strategy. The second two units are drawn from marketing, finance, human resources, localization, strategy, and international retailing. The last four units are earned by writing a dissertation.

For futher information on the program contact Dr. Steve Burt (Course Director) or Ms. Khlayre Mullin (Course Administrator) at the addresses given above.

University of Strathclyde

Strathclyde Graduate Business School
199 Cathedral Street
Glasgow G4 0QU

Degrees awarded:	MBA, MSc in Procurement Management
Areas of concentration:	General business
Admissions requirements:	Bachelor's degree, 3+ years work experience, GMAT, 24 years old or older
Media:	Traditional texts, other media may include video- and audiocassettes, software
Total units in program:	60 credits
Residency:	Four weekend residencies
Accreditation:	GAAP
Year founded:	1796
Ownership:	Nonprofit, state
Phone:	+44 (0)141 553 6167
Fax:	+44 (0)141 553 6137
E-mail:	m.mcrindle@.strath.ac.uk
Web site:	www.strath.ac.uk

Strathclyde offers the MBA and MSc in Procurement Management degrees via distance learning and residential programs. In the MBA program, extensive study guides are provided for each subject. Some courses are taught using videocassettes and other media, such as audiocassettes and computer software.

Each student is assigned a tutor with each course. Students are required to attend at least four weekend residencies at the business school during their period of study.

The MSc in Procurement Management degree is earned much as the MBA, with a two-year program culminating in a diploma and a third year to earn the Master's degree. This program bills itself as a distance program, but is designed more for British students, as several more weekend residencies are required.

For more information about the programs, contact Melissa McCrindle at the email or telephone number above.

University of Surrey

Surrey European Management School
Guildford
Surrey, GU2 5XH
United Kingdom

Degree awarded:	MBA
Area of concentration:	General business
Admissions requirements:	Bachelor's degree and 3 years management experience
Media:	Study guide, traditional texts, CD-ROM
Total units in program:	120 credits plus dissertation
Residency:	Not required, but strongly recommended
Accreditation:	GAAP, AACSB
Year founded:	1891
Ownership:	State
Phone:	(44-1483) 25-93-47
Fax:	(44-1483) 25-95-11
E-mail:	sems@surrey.ac.uk
Web site:	www.sems.surrey.ac.uk

Surrey's MBA consists of 6 core modules, 2 elective modules, and a dissertation. It may be completed in one year when studied on a full-time basis, or two years part-time. Each module involves assignments and projects, or written examinations. While no residency is required, review workshops prior to exams are strongly advised.

Surrey currently operates 10 distance-learning centers, and will consider opening another anywhere 25 qualified students are interested in undertaking the program. All MBA students, regardless of study mode, follow the same academic program, and are centrally assessed by the same professors.

Applicants without a Bachelor's degree or similar qualification will be considered for admission to the MBA upon satisfactory completion of the school's Open Access program, a primer course covering the basics of accounting, finance, statistics, marketing and management.

Open Access is taught through a series of modules designed for self-paced study. A tutor is assigned at the school to guide the student through the assignments. A final workshop takes place at the school on a Saturday, although on-site workshops can be arranged for corporations if several employees are participating. Once students complete the course they may move directly to the MBA program.

University of Texas at Dallas

Master of International Management Studies
Box 830688–LF16
Richardson, TX 75083-0688

Degrees awarded:	MBA, MA in international management
Areas of concentration:	International business, international management
Admissions requirements:	Bachelor's degree, essay, letter of recommendation, work experience, telephone interview
Media:	Video-, audio-, and computer conferencing, audiocassettes, computer software, Internet, traditional texts
Total units in program:	36 credit hours (MA), 48 credit hours (MBA)
Residency:	Four two-day sessions (both degrees)
Accreditation:	Regional, AACSB
Year founded:	1969
Ownership:	Nonprofit, state
Phone:	(972) 883-MIMS
Fax:	(972) 883-6164
E-mail:	glemba@utdallas.edu
Web site:	www.utdallas.edu/dept/mgmt/mims/mims.html

The university's MIMS program awards both an MA in international management and an MBA with a strong emphasis on international business. The MIMS program uses the Internet to deliver the curriculum through a variety of audio and video technologies. A substantial portion of the MIMS curriculum is delivered during four two-day retreats in a traditional lecture/seminar format and one ten-day foreign study tour (latter part of July).

The remainder of the curriculum is delivered to students at their location, using a variety of distance-learning technologies, such as Internet groupware, video-cassettes, and Internet-streamed audio files and slides. The Business Core portion of the curriculum is delivered entirely over the Internet.

Students successfully completing the business core (12 credit hours) and the MIMS curriculum (24 credit hours) receive a Master of Arts in international management studies. Students who wish to earn an MBA instead can take additional courses and receive the 49-credit-hour MBA.

A Bachelor's degree, essay of intent, one or more letters of recommendation, sufficient work experience, and access to the Internet are all prerequisites to the coursework.

University of Warwick

Distance Learning MBA Office
Warwick Business School
Coventry, CV4 7AL
United Kingdom

Degree awarded:	MBA
Area of concentration:	General business
Admissions requirements:	Bachelor's degree, 3 years work experience
Media:	Correspondence and e-mail, although computer work is not necessary
Total units in program:	Three parts plus a dissertation
Residency:	Three short residencies
Accreditation:	GAAP
Year founded:	1965
Ownership:	Nonprofit, state
Phone:	(44-1203) 524-100
Fax:	(44-1203) 524-411
E-mail:	pgadmissions@admin.warwick.ac.uk
Web site:	www.warwick.ac.uk/postgrad/social/wbs/mba-dl.htm

Warwick offers the MBA through a largely distance-learning format, although three "induction days" are required at the beginning of each of the program's three parts, plus one compulsory eight-day residential seminar. These residencies may be taken on campus in England or in Hong Kong, Singapore, or Malaysia. Exams are also held in these locations, but can be held elsewhere by special arrangement. Each year, Warwick's exams are held in as many as thirty countries worldwide.

A Bachelor's degree and three years of relevant work experience are required for entrance to the program. High GMAT scores may waive part of the requirements.

Students anywhere in the world may register with Warwick and then pursue the MBA from home, with the aid of a distance-learning course developed by Wolsey Hall, a private school that has for many years offered such courses for the University of London's external degrees. Access to a personal computer is desirable but not essential. The school offers telephone and e-mail tutorial support, and comprehensive correspondence study materials.

The main work in the program consists of completing assignments at the rate of two per month. Each student is assigned a tutor for each course. This person corrects the homework and is also available by phone for assistance and consultation. Tutors come from the Warwick staff or "another institution of higher education." The program is divided into three parts: In parts A and B, students cover core ideas and tools needed in business; part C gives individuals the chance to investigate further an area of special interest via in-depth electives. A thesis is written after completing these three parts.

The period of study is usually four years, roughly twelve hours a week, but it can be three years if the dissertation is completed during the final year of study. There is a free six-lesson course in essential study skills for those who have been away from academic learning for a while.

University of Western Ontario

Richard Ivey School of Business
London, ON N6A 3K7
Canada

Degree awarded:	MBA
Area of concentration:	General business
Admissions requirements:	Bachelor's degree or work-related education, GMAT, essay, letter of recommendation, work experience, employer approval
Media:	Videoconferencing
Total units in program:	22 credits
Residency:	Four one-week sessions on campus, plus regular classes at one of seven off-campus Canadian sites
Accreditation:	GAAP
Year founded:	1878
Ownership:	Nonprofit, state
Phone:	(519) 661-3277
Fax:	(519) 850-2341
E-mail:	tdeutsch@ivey.uwo.ca
Web site:	www.ivey.uwo.ca

The Ivey School of Business at the University of Western Ontario offers its Videoconference Executive MBA (VEMBA) to working professionals who are interested in a program that allows them to combine learning with daily applications to their current workplace. A Bachelor's degree is required for the program, but this requirement may be waived if sufficient work-related education can be proved. A minimum of eight years of business experience is required, and three of these should have been in a managerial position.

Off-site delivery centers in Vancouver, Edmonton, Calgary, London, Toronto, Ottawa and Montreal are linked with professors in the studio. Students in the videoconferenced program come together in one location, four times a year. The program is structured so that they spend as much time together in a common location as they do in electronic classrooms across the country. VEMBA classes are held on Friday and Saturday every second week, from mid-August to June. The program takes two years to complete.

Students at each of the delivery sites group into "learning teams" to compare work as the program progresses. The learning team analyzes cases, prepares presentations, and acts as a support group for individuals in the class. Professors may be contacted by mail, telephone, videoconferencing, e-mail, or fax, and Internet access may be required for certain periods of the program. Distance learners have access to Ivey's library, e-mail and computer network, and to many forms of student support including advising and career placement.

University of Westminster

Harrow Business School
Watford Road
Harrow, HA1 3TP
United Kingdom

Degree awarded:	MBA
Area of concentration:	Design management
Admissions requirements:	Bachelor's degree and three years work experience
Media:	Internet, CD-ROM
Total units in program:	Nine modules, a dissertation and oral presentation
Residency:	Opening workshop and several 4-day workshops
Accreditation:	GAAP
Year founded:	1838
Ownership:	Private
Phone:	(44-171) 911-5000
Fax:	(44-171) 911-5931
E-mail:	a.j.barratt@wmin.ac.uk
Web site:	www. mbadesign.co.uk

Westminster offers a distance MBA with a concentration in design management. The program is module-based, with a 4-day workshop for each module. The philosophy of the program is based on the idea that design is a critical strategic resource and that the effective management of design is a key factor in organization and competition.

The student body comprises practicing international designers from a wide range of design disciplines, as well as business managers and consultants. It is represented in the U.S. through a strategic collaboration with the Design Management Institute, which can be reached through www.dmi.org.

Students are assigned to "buddy groups" during the opening workshop. The group is intended to act as a means of sharing ideas and solving problems, both in the workshops themselves and while students are undertaking their private study. Each buddy group also has a tutor from the university academic staff, who is there to provide further support if needed.

The course contains a high proportion of distance learning over the Internet, enabling students to continue working while they study. Four-day workshops take place every ten weeks at the Harrow Business School in the U.K. or in Boston, Massachusetts, allowing review of the completed study packs, and an opportunity to apply the understanding gained to design management problems, to encourage sharing of ideas, experience and interaction among students.

Nine modules are completed for the degree. Each module contains a minor and a major assignment, which are completed within the 10-week cycle assigned to that subject area. Students must also undertake a Master's dissertation, which is submitted twenty weeks after completion of the final module, and is supported by an oral presentation.

A Bachelor's degree and three years of professional experience are required for the program. Extensive work experience will be taken into account.

University of Wisconsin–Whitewater

On-Line MBA
4033 Carlson Hall
College of Business and Economics
Whitewater, WI 53190

Degree awarded:	MBA
Areas of concentration:	Finance, management, marketing
Admissions requirements:	Bachelor's degree, GMAT
Media:	Internet
Total units in program:	36 credits
Residency:	None
Accreditation:	Regional, AACSB
Year founded:	1868
Ownership:	Nonprofit, state
Phone:	(414) 472-1945
Fax:	(414) 472-4863
E-mail:	zahnd@uwwvax.uww.edu
Web site:	www.uww.edu/business/onlinemba/

A wholly on-line MBA, which requires students to have a Pentium processor, modem, CD-ROM drive, and Windows operating system. The emphases offered are finance, management, and marketing. Other concentrations are available through a combination of on-line study and residency, and include health care and international business. Faculty contact is by telephone, fax and e-mail, and the university makes a point of its faculty being interested in a high level of student contact.

Admission to the program is granted to students with a Bachelor's degree and GMAT scores. A GPA of 2.9 or higher during undergraduate studies is also needed to enter the program, but different combinations of GPA scores and GMAT scores will allow admission as well. Check the web site for equations.

In the program, students learn how individual, team, and organization-level behavior affects organizational operations. The case method approach develops skills in collecting, analyzing, and interpreting data. Students also improve their abilities to conceptualize, evaluate, and implement solutions as necessary in addressing complex, unstructured business problems. The 36-credit MBA uses a program called Learning Space to deliver all course materials on-line.

Professional accreditation is from the International Association for Management Education (AACSB).

Worcester Polytechnic Institute

Advanced Distance Learning Network
100 Institute Road
Worcester, MA 01609

Degree awarded:	MBA
Areas of concentration:	Management of technology, management of information systems, technology marketing, technological innovation, and operations management.
Admissions requirements:	Bachelor's degree, good understanding of computer systems, Internet access, three semesters of college-level math or two of calculus
Media:	Interactive compressed video, Express-Mailed videocassettes, Internet
Total units in program:	49 credits
Residency:	None
Accreditation:	Regional, AACSB
Year founded:	1865
Ownership:	Independent, nonprofit
Phone:	(508) 831-5220
Fax:	(508) 831-5720
E-mail:	adln@wpi.edu
Web site:	www.wpi.edu/Academics/ADLN

The Department of Management at WPI has been involved with technology-based management distance education since 1979, when the school developed its Advanced Distance Learning Network (ADLN). ADLN courses consist of the same content and materials as on-campus meetings, although instructional methods are sometimes altered to suit the mode of delivery. Class meetings originate in one of WPI's studio classrooms, and are delivered to ADLN students via interactive compressed video, Express-Mailed videocassettes or the Internet, depending on the resources available to the student. Materials such as books, handouts and supplemental readings are Express-Mailed, faxed, e-mailed, or posted to the Web.

The applications-oriented, technology-focused MBA program is designed to provide students with the "big picture" perspective required of successful upper-level managers, and the hands-on knowledge needed to meet the daily demands of the workplace. A strong emphasis on behavioral skills prepares students to be leaders in any organization and the global threads throughout the curriculum ensure an understanding of the global imperative facing all businesses.

The MBA focuses on the management of technology and features a highly integrative curriculum that emphasizes leadership, ethics, communication, and a global perspective. This 49-credit MBA program may be reduced to as few as 31 credits with an appropriate academic background. Prior to waivers, this equates to 9 foundation courses, 5 core courses, 12 credits from electives, and a 3-credit graduate qualifying project in which the student applies the skills learned from the program in an actual business setting. In addition to the MBA, the Department of Management at WPI also offers a 15-credit Graduate Management Certificate option for individuals wishing to pursue graduate coursework, without committing to a full degree program.

All students admitted to a graduate management degree or certificate program are assigned a faculty advisor and must file a curriculum plan during their first year in the program. Depending on prior academic background, part-time students typically complete the MBA program in three to five years, while full-time students may finish in as little as one year.

Appendix A: Schools Offering Regional Distance Degrees

Some schools offer distance learning, but only to students within their state, or local area. The reason may be lack of funds or faculty, technological limitations, or simply that they aren't set up to deal with students from around the globe. Here are 23 such schools, sorted by region. If you live in the region served, such a school may well be a good option, as you can have closer contact with faculty and fellow students. Oftentimes, the courses are sent via compressed video to off-site learning centers, and students are required to attend on a schedule. Contact the schools or view their web sites for such details.

Arkansas

University of Arkansas at Little Rock
College of Business Administration
2801 South University Avenue
Little Rock, AR 72204
Phone: (501) 569-3356
Fax: (501) 569-8898
E-mail: talawrence@ualr.edu
Web site: www.ualr.edu
MBA offered by distance learning to students in the state of Arkansas.

California

San Jose State University
Business Graduate Programs
One Washington Square—BT250
San Jose, CA 95192-0162
Phone: (408) 924-3420
Fax: (408) 924-3426
E-mail: bmba@cob.sjsu.edu
Web site: www.cob.sjsu.edu
Master of Science in transportation management (MSTM) offered by distance learning to students in the state of California.

Illinois

Southern Illinois University at Edwardsville
Box 1051
Edwardsville, IL 62026-1051
Phone: (618) 650-3979
E-mail: fmarti@siue.edu
Web site: www.siue.edu/BUSINESS
MBA offered by distance learning to students in the state of Illinois.

University of Illinois at Springfield
Department of Management Information Systems
P.O. Box 19243
Springfield, IL 62794
Phone: (217) 206-6067
Fax: (217) 206-7543
E-mail: simpson.nancy@uis.edu
MA in management of information systems offered by distance learning to students in the state of Illinois.

Indiana

University of Notre Dame
Executive MBA Program
126 College of Business
Notre Dame, IN 46556-5646
Phone: (219) 631- 5285
Fax: (219) 631-6783
E-mail: barry.vandyck.1@nd.edu
Executive MBA available through learning sites in Indianapolis, Indiana; Hoffman Estates, Illinois; and Toledo, Ohio.

Iowa

Drake University
College of Business and Public Administration
Des Moines, IA 50311
Phone: (515) 271-2188
Fax: (515) 271-4518
E-mail: cbpa.gradprograms@drake.edu
Web site: www.drake.edu/cbpa/graduate/mba.edu
MBA offered by distance learning to students in Iowa who have been admitted to a Master's degree program or who already hold a Master's degree.

Maryland

Bowie State University
School of Continuing Education
14000 Jericho Park Road
Bowie, MD 20715
Phone: (301) 464-6586
Fax: (301) 464-7786
E-mail: ibrandon@bowiestate.edu
MS offered by distance learning at delivery sites in Essex, Laurel, and Reisterstown.

University of Baltimore
1420 North Charles Street
Baltimore, MD 21201
Phone: (410) 837-4953
Fax: (410) 837-5652
E-mail: rfrederick@ubmail.ubalt.edu
MBA offered by distance learning to students in the state of Maryland.

Michigan

Lake Superior State University
650 West Easterday
Sault Sainte Marie, MI 49783
Phone: (888) 800-LSSU, Ext. 2554
Fax: (906) 635-2762
E-mail: scamp@lakers.lssu.edu
Web site: www.lssu.edu
MBA offered by distance learning to students in the state of Michigan.

Minnesota

College of St. Scholastica
1200 Kenwood Avenue
Duluth, MN 55811
Phone: (218) 723-6415
Fax: (218) 723-6290
E-mail: pjones@css.edu
Web site: www.css.edu
MA offered by distance learning to regional students.

Mississippi

Mississippi State University
Division of Continuing Education
PO Box 5247
Mississippi State, MS 39762-5247
Phone: (662) 325-1891
Fax: (662) 325-8666
E-mail: wcole@ce.msstate.edu

University of Southern Mississippi
Graduate Business Programs
P.O. Box 5096
Hattiesburg, MS 39406
Phone: (601) 266-5050
Fax: (601) 266-4639
E-mail: king@cba.usm.edu
MS offered by distance learning to students in the state of Mississippi.

Nebraska

Chadron State College
Dept. of Education
Chadron, NE 69337
Phone: (308) 432-6210 • (800) 600-3055
Fax: (308) 432-6473
E-mail: dsmith@csc.edu
Web site: www.csc.edu/schools/idl/cscidl.html
This distance-learning MBA is available to residents of 25 counties in western and central Nebraska. Instruction is provided via on-campus courses televised to seven remote sites.

University of Nebraska-Lincoln
College of Business Administration 126
Lincoln, NE 68588-0405
Phone: (402) 472-2338
Fax: (402) 472-5180
E-mail: gradadv@cbamail.unl.edu
Web site: www.unl.edu/conted/telecom/index.html
Nebraska students may earn an MBA through workplace-delivered materials.

New Mexico

Eastern New Mexico University
Station 49
Portales, NM 88130
Phone: (505) 562-2166
Fax: (505) 562-2168
E-mail: a.schreoder@enmu.edu
Web site: www.enmu.edu
The distance-learning MBA degree offered by Eastern New Mexico University is available solely to students in southeastern New Mexico.

New York

Alfred University
College of Business
Saxon Drive
Alfred, NY 14802
Phone: (607) 871-2626
Fax: (607) 871-2114
E-mail: facton@bigvax.alfred.edu
Web site: www.alfred.edu
MBA offered by distance learning to students in the local area.

North Dakota

North Dakota State University
P.O. Box 5137
Putnam Hall
Fargo, ND 58105
Phone: (701) 231-7681
Fax: (701) 231-7508
E-mail: pabrown@plains.nodak.edu
Web site: www.ndsu.nodak.edu/cba/
MBA offered by distance learning to students in the state of North Dakota.

University of North Dakota
Box 8098
Grand Forks, ND 58202-8098
Phone: (701) 777-2975
Fax: (701) 777-2019
E-mail: wambsgan@badlands.nodak.edu
Web site: www.und.nodak.edu
MBA offered by distance learning to students in the state of North Dakota.

Ohio

The University of Akron
259 South Broadway
Room 412
Akron, OH 44325-4805
Phone: (330) 972-7043
Fax: (330) 972-6588
E-mail: jwilliams@uakron.edu
Web site: www.uakron.edu/cba/
MBA offered by distance learning to students regionally.

Oklahoma

Cameron University
School of Graduate and Professional Studies
2800 Gore Boulevard
Lawton, OK 73505
Phone: (580) 581-2986
Fax: (580) 581-5532
E-mail: graduate@cameron.edu
Web site: www.cameron.edu/academic/graduate/business/mba.html
MBA offered by distance learning to local students admitted to the graduate school.

Pennsylvania

Pennsylvania State University at Erie
The Behrend College
Continuing and Distance Education Office
5091 Station Road
Erie, PA 16563
Phone: (814) 898-6100
Fax: (814) 898-6044
E-mail: jub9@psu.edu
Web site: www.pserie.psu.edu
MBA offered by distance learning to students who attend class at Jamestown Community College in Jamestown, New York.

South Carolina

University of South Carolina
MBA Office
College of Business Administration
Columbia, SC 29208
Phone: (803) 777-7940
Fax: (803) 777-9018
E-mail: mba@darla.badm.sc.edu
Web site: www.badm.sc.edu/mba/
MBA offered statewide by distance learning. Students must attend 14 Saturday sessions on campus.

Tennessee

East Tennessee State University
Box 70699
Johnson City, TN 37614
Phone: (423) 439-5314
E-mail: greenr@etsu.edu
Web site: www.etsu.edu/scs/distedu.htm
MBA by distance learning offered locally to students participating in cohort groups.

Texas

Amber University
1700 Eastgate Drive
Garland, Texas 75041
Phone: (972) 279-6511, Ext. 135
Fax: (972) 279-9773
E-mail: webteam@amberu.edu
Web site: amberu.edu.
MA offered by distance learning to students in the state of Texas.

Appendix B: Schools Offering a Bachelor's in Business Administration by Distance Learning

In the interest of providing a wide range of options for distance scholars interested in business fields, we offer this list of 55 accredited institutions offering an undergraduate business administration degree (almost always a BBA). These schools may also provide a useful resource for those who wish to add to their business knowledge or fulfill prerequisites prior to enrolling in an MBA program. If, for instance, a program requires you to have taken undergraduate marketing, or statistics, or accounting, or any of a number of other similar fields commonly required, you can fulfill the requirement conveniently, through distance learning.

Athabasca University
Information Centre
1 University Drive
Athabasca, AB T9S 3A3
Canada
Phone: (800) 788-9041
Fax: (403) 675-6145
E-mail: auinfo@athabascau.ca.
Web site: www.athabascau.ca.

Atlantic Union College
Assistant to the Director
P.O. Box 1000
South Lancaster, MA 01561
Phone: (978) 368-2300
Fax: (978) 368-2015

Baker College On-Line
Director of Development
1050 West Bristol Road
Flint, MI 48507
Phone: (800) 621-7440
Fax: (810) 766-4399
E-mail: online@baker.edu
Web site: www.baker.edu

Bellevue University
Admissions Counselor
1000 Galvin Road South
Bellevue, NE 68005
Phone: (800) 756-7920
Fax: (402) 293-2020
E-mail: dij@scholars.bellevue.edu
Web site: bruins.bellevue.edu

Caldwell College
Corporate and Adult Admissions
9 Ryerson Avenue
Caldwell, NJ 07006
Phone: (973) 228-4424
Fax: (973) 228-2897
E-mail: caldwellad@aol.com

Central Michigan University
Independent and Distance Learning Center
Rowe 126
Mount Pleasant, MI 48859
Phone: (800) 950-1144
Fax: (517) 774-3537
E-mail: infocntr@cmich.edu
Web site: www.cel.cmich.edu

Central Washington University
Academic Advising Office
400 East 8th Avenue
Ellensburg, WA 98926
Phone: (509) 963-1504
Fax: (509) 963-1590
E-mail: lyndeg@cwu.edu
Web Site: www.cwu.edu

Champlain College
Registrar
Continuing Education Division
163 South Willard Street
Burlington, VT 05402
Phone: (802) 860-2777
Fax: (802) 860-2774
E-mail: ced@champlain.edu
Web site: www.champlain.edu/success

City University
Advisor for Distance Learning
919 Southwest Grady Way
2nd Floor
Renton, WA 98055
Phone: (800) 426-5596
Fax: (425) 277-2437
E-mail: info@cityu.edu
Web site: www.cityu.edu

Clarkson College
Coordinator of Distance Education
101 South 42nd Street
Omaha, NE 68131
Phone: (402) 552-3037
Fax: (402) 552-6058
E-mail: ajrami@clrkcol.crhsnet.edu
Web site: www.clarksoncollege.edu

The College of West Virginia
Student Outreach Coordinator
P.O. Box AG
Beckley, WV 25802-2830
Phone: (304) 253-7351
Fax: (304) 253-3485
E-mail: saell@cwv.edu
Web site: www.cwv.edu/saell/index.html

Eastern New Mexico University
Director of Extended Learning
Station 49
Portales, NM 88130
Phone: (505) 562-2166
Fax: (505) 562-2168
E-mail: a.schroeder@enmu.edu
Web site: www.enmu.edu

Eastern Oregon University
Director, Distance Learning
Zabel Hall
1410 L Avenue
La Grande, OR 97850-2899
Phone: (541) 962-3614
Fax: (541) 962-3627
E-mail: jhart@eosc.osshe.edu
Web site: www.eosc.osshe.edu/dep

Empire State College
State University of New York
Marketing Assistant
Center for Distance Learning
28 Union Avenue
Saratoga Springs, NY 12866
Phone: (518) 587-2660
E-mail: cdl@secva.esc.edu

Fort Hays State University
Assistant Dean of Continuing Education
600 Park Street
Hays, KS 67601
Phone: (785) 628-4291
Fax: (785) 628-4037
Web site: www.fhsu.edu

Griggs University
Director of Admissions/Registrar
P.O. Box 4437
Silver Spring, MD 20914-4437
Phone: (301) 680-6579
Fax: (301) 680-6577
E-mail: 74617.3274@compuserve.com
Web site: www.hsi.edu

Hampton University
Administrative Assistant to the Dean
College of Continuing Education
Hampton, VA 23668
Phone: (757) 727-5773
Fax: (757) 727-5949

Lake Superior State University
Director of Continuing Education
844 North Campus Court
Sault Sainte Marie, MI 49783
Phone: (906) 635-2554
Fax: (906) 635-2762
E-mail: scamp@lakers.lssu.edu
Web site: www.lssu.edu

Liberty University
1971 University Boulevard
Lynchburg, VA 24502
Phone: (800) 424-9595
Fax: (804) 628-7977
E-mail: webmaster@liberty.edu
Web site: www.liberty.edu

Marywood University
Director of Distance Education
2300 Adams Avenue
Scranton, PA 18509
Phone: (570) 348-6235
Fax: (570) 961-4751
E-mail: pmunk@ac.marywood.edu
Web site: www.marywood.edu

Mercy College
Admissions Coordinator
555 Broadway
Dobbs Ferry, NY 10522
Phone: (800) MERCY-NY
Fax: (914) 674-7382
E-mail: admission@merlin.mercynet.edu
Web site: www.merlin.mercynet.edu

Morehead State University
Accounting and Economics
222 Combs Building
Morehead, KY 40351
Phone: (606) 783-2151
Fax: (606) 783-5025
E-mail: g.miller@morehead-st.edu
Web site: www.morehead-st.edu

Mount Saint Vincent University
Open Learning Program Coordinator
Halifax, NS B3M 2J6
Canada
Phone: (902) 457-6511
Fax: (902) 457-2618
E-mail: Carolyn.Nobes@msvu.ca

New Mexico State University
Director of Distance Education
Box 3 WEC
Las Cruces, NM 88003
Phone: (505) 646-5837
Fax: (505) 646-2044
E-mail: lames@nmsu.edu
Web site: www.nmsu.edu

New York Institute of Technology
Dean
P.O. Box 2029
Central Islip, NY 11722-9029
Phone: (800) 222-NYIT
Fax: (516) 348-3399
Web site: www.nyit.edu

Northern Arizona University
Continuing Education
P.O. Box 04117
Flagstaff, AZ 86011
Phone: (520) 523-4212
Fax: (520) 523-1169
Web site: www.nau.edu

Northwood University
Provost of University College
3225 Cook Road
Midland, MI 48640-2398
Phone: (517) 837-4455
Fax: (517) 837-4457
Web site: www.northwood.edu

Old Dominion University
Associate Director of Distance Learning
Education Building, Room 145
Norfolk, VA 23529
Phone: (757) 683-3163
Fax: (757) 683-5492
E-mail: jpkl00f@eagle.cc.odu.edu
Web site: www.odu.edu

Oral Roberts University
Director of Correspondence Studies
7777 South Lewis Avenue
Tulsa, OK 74171
Phone: (918) 495-6238
Fax: (918) 495-7695
E-mail: slle@oru.edu
Web site: www.oru.edu/slle/

Regents College
Outreach Coordinator
7 Columbia Circle
Albany, NY 12203
Phone: (518) 464-8611
Fax: (518) 464-8777
Web site: www.regents.edu

Regis University
Program Representative
7600 East Orchard Road, Suite 100N
Englewood, CO 80111
Phone: (303) 458-3560
Fax: (303) 694-1554
E-mail: spsdean@regis.edu
Web site: www.regis.edu

Roger Williams University
Department Coordinator
Open Program
1 Old Ferry Road
Bristol, RI 02809
Phone: (401) 254-3037
Fax: (401) 254-3560
E-mail: tjc@alph.rwu.edu
Web site: www.rwu.edu

Rutgers
Director of Continuing Education and
    Summer Sessions
249 University-Blumenthal 208
Newark, NJ 07102
Phone: (973) 648-5760
Fax: (973) 648-1587
E-mail: csrusso@andromeda.rutgers.edu
Web site: www.rutgers.edu

Saint Joseph's College
Admissions Office
Department 840
278 White's Bridge Road
Standish, ME 04084-5263
Phone: (800) 752-4723
Fax: (207) 892-7480
E-mail: gcarro@sjcme.edu
Web site: www.sjcme.edu

Saint Mary-of-the-Woods College
WED Admissions Director
Saint Mary-of-the-Woods, IN 47876
Phone: (812) 535-5107
Fax: (812) 535-5186
E-mail: wedadms@woods.smwc.edu
Web site: www.woods.smwc.edu

Salve Regina University
Director, Extension Study
100 Ochre Point Avenue
Newport, RI 02840
Phone: (800) 637-0002
Fax: (401) 849-0702
E-mail: mistol@salve.edu
Web site: www.salve.edu

Southern Oregon University
Associate Director
Extended Learning Programs
1250 Siskiyou Boulevard
Ashland, OR 97520
Phone: (541) 552-6517
Fax: (541) 552-6047
E-mail: scott@sou.edu

Southern Polytechnic State University
Program Director
1100 South Marietta Parkway
Marietta, GA 30060
Phone: (770) 528-7317
Fax: (770) 528-5511
E-mail: jmckee@spsu.edu
Web site: www.spsu.edu

Southern Utah University
Chair, Department of Business
351 West Center Street
Cedar City, UT 84720
Phone: (435) 865-7784
E-mail: groesbeck@suu.edu
Web site: www.suu.edu

Southwestern Adventist University
Director
Adult Degree Program
P.O. Box 567
Keene, TX 76059
Phone: (888) 732-7928
Fax: (817) 556-4742
E-mail: adpsec@swau.edu
Web site: www.swau.edu

Southwestern Assemblies of God University
Enrollment Counselor
1200 Sycamore Street
Waxahachie, TX 75165-2342
Phone: (972) 937-4010
Fax: (972) 923-0488
E-mail: stiger@sagu.edu
Web site: www.sagu.edu

Southwest State University
Dean
North Highway 23
Marshall, MN 56258
Phone: (507) 537-6108
Fax: (507) 537-6200

Stephens College
Academic Services Coordinator
Campus Box 2083
1200 East Broadway
Columbia, MO 65215
Phone: (800) 388-7579
Fax: (573) 876-7248
E-mail: mc_stu@wc.stephens.edu
Web site: www.stephens.edu

Thomas Edison State College
Director of Admissions
Office of Admissions
101 West State Street
Trenton, NJ 08608
Phone: (609) 984-1150
Fax: (609) 984-8447
E-mail: info@tesc.edu
Web site: www.tesc.edu

University of Alaska Southeast
Assistant to the Dean
11120 Glacier Highway
Juneau, AK 99801
Phone: (907) 465-6353
Fax: (907) 465-6383
E-mail: jnsdg@acad1.alaska.edu
Web site: www.uas.alaska.edu

University of Great Falls
Telecommunications Office
1301 20th Street, South
Great Falls, MT 59405
Phone: (406) 791-5321
Fax: (406) 791-5394
Web site: www.ugf.edu

University of Houston
Distance Education Advisor
4242 South Mason Road
Katy, TX 77450
Phone: (281) 395-2800
Fax: (281) 395-2629
E-mail: deadvisor@uh.edu
Web site: www.uh.edu

University of Mary
Dean
7500 University Drive
Bismarck, ND 58504
Phone: (701) 255-7500
Fax: (701) 255-7687
Web site: www.umary.edu

University of Maryland University College
Enrollment Team
Undergraduate Student Services
University Boulevard at Adelphi Road
College Park, MD 20742-1636
Phone: (800) 283-6832
Fax: (301) 985-7364
E-mail: distance@nova.umuc.edu
Web site: www.umuc.edu/distance/bdaad.html

University of North Dakota
CEDP Coordinator
Division of Continuing Education
Box 9021
Grand Forks, ND 58202-9021
Phone: (800) 342-8230
Fax: (701) 777-4282
E-mail: lynette_krenelka@mail.und.nodak.edu

University of Phoenix
Enrollment Department
100 Spear Street, Suite 110
San Francisco, CA 94105
Phone: (800) 742-4742
Fax: (415) 541-7832
Web site: www.uophx.edu/online

University of Windsor
Continuing Education Office
401 Sunset Avenue
Windsor, ON N9B 3P4
Canada
Phone: (519) 253-3000, Ext. 3305
Fax: (519) 973-7038
Web site: www.uwindsor.ca/coned/index.html

University of Wisconsin-Platteville
Director
Extended Degree in Business
506 Pioneer Tower
1 University Plaza
Platteville, WI 53818
Phone: (800) 362-3654
Fax: (608) 342-1466
E-mail: adams@uwplatte.edu
Web site: www.uwplatte.edu/edp

Upper Iowa University
Director
External Degree Programs
P.O. Box 1861
Fayette, IA 52142
Phone: (319) 425-5283
Fax: (319) 425-5353
E-mail: extdegree@uiu.edu
Web site: www.uiu.edu

Utah State University
Staff Assistant
UMC 3720
Logan, UT 84322-3720
Phone: (435) 707-2079
Fax: (435) 797 1399
E-mail: m.lyon@ce.usu.edu
Web site: www.usu.edu

Appendix C: Correspondence Courses

The following schools offer graduate-level courses in MBA-related fields. This may be useful for a couple of reasons. First, some of the schools listed in this book allow students to transfer in prior credits. You may wish to take a few correspondence courses in business administration or related fields before making the big jump to enrolling in an MBA program. In addition, most MBA programs assume a certain baseline knowledge of math, statistics, business concepts, and so forth. You can fill in the gaps with correspondence courses, further ensuring your success when you begin your MBA program. For details, including costs, delivery method (many courses are offered on-line these days, in addition to, or instead of, by traditional correspondence), and requirements, contact the schools directly.

Aurora University
School of Business and Professional Studies
347 South Gladstone Avenue
Aurora, IL 60506-4892
Phone: (630) 844-4888
Fax: (630) 844-7830
E-mail: lquick@admin.aurora.edu
Web site: www.aurora.edu

Graduate-level courses in financial management/planning, human resources, leadership, marketing, production management, and quality management.

Ball State University
College of Business-WB 146
Muncie, IN 47306
Phone: (765) 285-1931
Fax: (765) 285-8818
E-mail: bsumba@bsuvc.bsu.edu
Web site: www.bsu.edu/business/mba

Graduate-level courses in accounting, business law, economics, finance, management, manufacturing management, and marketing.

Bowie State University
Department of Business and Economics
School of Continuing Education
14000 Jericho Park Road
Bowie, MD 20715
Phone: (301) 464-6586
Fax: (301) 464-7786
E-mail: ida.brandon@bowiestate.edu

Graduate-level courses in management, management information systems, and public and private management.

Cameron University
School of Graduate and Professional Studies
2800 Gore Boulevard
Lawton, OK 73505
Phone: (580) 581-2986
Fax: (580) 581-5532
E-mail: graduate@cameron.edu
Web site:
www.cameron.edu/academic/graduate/busin ess/mba.html

Graduate-level courses in accounting, business ethics, economics, finance, management, management information systems, marketing, and organizational management. In addition, noncredit courses are available in accounting, business ethics, economics, finance, management, management information systems, marketing, and organizational management.

Charter Oak State College
Academic Affairs
66 Cedar Street
Newington, CT 06111-2646
Phone: (860) 666-4595
Fax: (860) 666-4852
E-mail: info@cosc.edu
Web site: www.cosc.edu

One graduate-level mathematics course.

City University
Admissions and Student Affairs
919 Southwest Grady Way
Renton, WA 98055
Phone: (800) 426-5596
Fax: (425) 277-2437
E-mail: info@cityu.edu

Graduate-level courses available in finance, management, and organizational behavior/development.

College of Insurance
Center for Professional Education
101 Murray Street
New York, NY 10007-2165
Phone: (212) 815-9232
Fax: (212) 964-3381
E-mail: tmarro@tcl.edu

Graduate-level courses in insurance and risk management.

College of St. Scholastica
Management Department Coordinator
1200 Kenwood Avenue
Duluth, MN 55811
Phone: (218) 723-6415
Fax: (218) 723-6290
E-mail: pjones@css.edu
Web site: www.css.edu

Graduate-level courses in finance and operations management.

Colorado State University
Distance Degree Program
Division of Educational Outreach
Spruce Hall
Fort Collins, CO 80523-1040
Phone: (970) 491-5288
Fax: (970) 491-7885
E-mail: info@learn.colostate.edu
Web site: www.colostate.edu/depts/CE

Graduate-level courses in accounting, finance, management, and marketing.

Eastern College
Business Department
1300 Eagle Road
St. Davids, PA 19087-3696
Phone: (610) 341-5972
Fax: (610) 341-1466
E-mail: gradadm@eastern.edu
Web site: www.eastern.edu

Graduate-level courses in developmental economics, economics, finance, management, and strategic management.

Eastern New Mexico University
College of Business
Station 49
Portales, NM 88130
Phone: (505) 562-2737
Fax: (505) 562-4331
E-mail: gerry.huybregts@enmu.edu
Web site: www.enmu.edu

Graduate-level courses in accounting, business policy/strategy, economics, finance, marketing, operations management, and organizational behavior/development.

East Tennessee State University
College of Business
Box 70699
Johnson City, TN 37614
Phone: (423) 439-5314
Fax: (423) 439-5770
E-mail: greenr@etsu.edu
Web site: www.etsu.edu/scs/distedu.htm

Graduate-level courses in management and marketing.

Edith Cowan University
Admissions Coordinator
External Studies
P.O. Box 830
Claremont, West Australia 6010
Australia
Phone: (61-8) 944-21460
E-mail: u.walter@cowan.edu.au

Graduate-level courses in management and management information systems. In addition, noncredit courses are offered in the same subject areas.

Embry-Riddle Aeronautical University
Director, Independent Studies
600 South Clyde Morris Boulevard
Daytona Beach, FL 32114
Phone: (904) 226-6397 • (800) 359-3728
Fax: (904) 226-7627
E-mail: indstudy@cts.db.erau.edu
Web site: www.db.erau.edu

Graduate courses in management information systems, aviation labor relations, and airport management.

Golden Gate University
536 Mission Street
San Francisco, CA 94105
Phone: (415) 442-7060
Fax: (415) 896-2394
E-mail: ssahni@ggu.edu
Web site: www.cybercampus.ggu.edu

Graduate-level courses in arts administration/management, finance, management, management information systems, marketing, organizational behavior/development, and taxation.

Heriot-Watt University
c/o Financial Times Management, Inc.
Two World Trade Center, Suite 1700
New York, NY 10048
Phone: (800) 622-9661
Fax: (212) 344-3469
E-mail: info@hwmba.net
Web site: www.hwmba.edu

Graduate-level courses in accounting, economics, finance, marketing, organizational behavior/development, quantitative analysis, and strategic management.

ISIM University
501 South Cherry Street, Suite 356
Denver, CO 80246
Phone: (303) 333-4224
Fax: (303) 336-1144
E-mail: admissions@isimu.edu
Web site: www.isimu.edu

Graduate-level courses in management and management information systems.

Kettering University
Office of Graduate Studies
1700 West Third Avenue
Flint, MI 48504-4898
Phone: (810) 762-7494
Fax: (810) 762-9935
E-mail: bbedore@kettering.edu
Web site: www.gmi.edu/official/acad/grad

One graduate-level course in manufacturing management.

Lake Superior State University
School of Business
650 West Easterday Avenue
Sault Sainte Marie, MI 49783
Phone: (888) 800-LSSU, ext. 2554
Fax: (906) 635-2762
E-mail: scamp@lakers.lssu.edu
Web site: www.lssu.edu

Graduate-level courses in advertising, business communications, business policy/strategy, finance, international business, management, management information systems, and public management.

Lehigh University
MBA Program
Rauch Business Center, Room 195
621 Taylor Street
Bethlehem, PA 18015
Phone: (610) 758-3418
Fax: (610) 758-5283
E-mail: kat3@lehigh.edu
Web site: www.lehigh.edu/~incbe/incbe.html

Graduate-level courses in accounting, advertising, business information science, business law, decision sciences, economics, finance, management, and management information systems. In addition, noncredit courses are available in the same subject areas.

Lesley College
School of Management
29 Everett Street
Cambridge, MA 02138
Phone: (617) 349-8656
Fax: (617) 349-8678
E-mail: rjette@lesley.edu
Web site: www.lesley.edu/som.html

Graduate-level courses in business ethics and human resources.

Madonna University
Cohort Online Programs
School of Business
36600 Schoolcraft Road
Livonia, MI 48150
Phone: (734) 432-5354
Fax: (734) 492-5364
E-mail: neuhause@smpt.munet.edu
Web site: www.munet.edu

Graduate-level courses in accounting, management information systems, organizational behavior/development, and strategic management.

Maharishi University of Management
Distance MBA Program
1600 North Fourth Street
Fairfield, IA 52557
Phone: (515) 472-1216
Fax: (515) 472-1191
E-mail: mba@mum.edu
Web site: www.mum.edu/SBPA/distance.html

Graduate-level courses in accounting, banking, finance, human resources, international business, management, management information systems, and marketing. These courses may also be taken on an audit basis.

Monash University
MBA Admissions
P.O. Box 2224
Caulfield Junction, Victoria, 3161
Australia
Phone: (61) 392151850
Fax: (61) 392151821
E-mail: genmba@mteliza.edu.au

Graduate-level courses in business ethics and international business. These courses may be taken for credit or no credit.

National-Louis University
Office of Continuing Education
1000 Capitol Drive
Wheeling, IL 60090
Phone: (800) 443-5522, ext. 5495
Fax: (847) 465-0593
E-mail: gext@wheeling1.nl.edu
Web site: www.nluconted.edu

Graduate and noncredit courses available in management information systems.

Naval Postgraduate School
Systems Management Department
555 Dyer Road, Building 330
CODE SM/Fa
Monterey, CA 93943
Phone: (831) 656-2756
Fax: (831) 656-3407
E-mail: gthomas@nps.navy.mil

One graduate-level course available in contract management.

New York Institute of Technology
School of Management
P.O. Box 8000
Old Westbury, NY 11568
Phone: (800) 345-NYIT
Fax: (516) 686-7613
E-mail: gberman@iris.nyit.edu
Web site: www.nyit.edu

Graduate-level courses in accounting, finance, international business, management information systems, and marketing.

North Dakota State University
P.O. Box 5137
Putnam Hall
Fargo, ND 58105
Phone: (701) 231-7681
Fax: (701) 231-7508
E-mail: pabrown@plains.nodak.edu
Web site: www.ndsu.nodak.edu/cba

Graduate-level courses in finance, human resources, managerial economics, and operations management.

Old Dominion University
TELETECHNET
Norfolk, VA 23529
Phone: (757) 683-3163
E-mail: jkline@odu.edu
Web site: www.odu.edu

Graduate-level courses in accounting, city/urban administration, economics, finance, information management, management, marketing, operations management, and taxation.

Open University of the Netherlands
Department of Economics, Public and
  Business Administration
Valkenburgerweg 167
Heerlen, 6419 AT
Netherlands
Phone: (045) 5762404
Fax: (045) 5762103
E-mail: ron.tuninga@ouh.nl

Graduate-level courses in accounting, business policy/strategy, commerce, economics, European business studies, financial management/planning, international business, and international marketing.

Regent University
School of Business
1000 Regent University Drive
Virginia Beach, VA 23464
Phone: (800) 477-3642
Fax: (757) 226-4369
E-mail: busschool@regent.edu
Web site: www.regent.edu

Graduate-level courses in accounting, entrepreneurship, finance, management, marketing, and nonprofit management.

Rensselaer Polytechnic Institute
Lally School of Management and Technology
C11 4011
Troy, NY 12180
Phone: (518) 276-7787
Fax: (518) 276-8026
E-mail: katchc@rpi.edu
Web site: lallyschool.rpi.edu

Graduate-level courses in accounting, business ethics, economics, finance, management, managerial economics, manufacturing management, and technology management.

Salve Regina University
Director, Extension Study
100 Ochre Point Avenue
Newport, RI 02840
Phone: (401) 847-6650 • (800) 637-0002
Fax: (401) 849-0702
E-mail: mistol@salve.edu
Web site: www.salve.edu

Graduate-level courses in management and management information systems.

Strayer University
Strayer Online
8382-F Terminal Road
Lorton, VA 22079
Phone: (703) 339-1850
Fax: (703) 339-1852
E-mail: jet@strayer.edu
Web site: www.strayer.edu

Graduate-level courses in accounting, business communications, economics, financial management/planning, information management, management information systems, operations management, organizational behavior/development, quantitative analysis, and strategic management.

Syracuse University
Director
Distance Education and Executive Education
700 University Avenue
Syracuse, NY 13244
Phone: (315) 443-3480 • (800) 442-0501
Fax: (315) 443-4174
E-mail: suisdp@syr.edu
Web site: www.syr.edu

Graduate-level courses in accounting, finance, management, managerial control, managerial dynamics, and marketing.

Temple University
School of Business and Management—MBA
Speakman Hall, Room 5
1810 North 13th Street
Philadelphia, PA 19122
Phone: (215) 204-4563
Fax: (215) 204-8300
E-mail: linda@sbm.temple.edu
Web site: www.sbm.temple.edu

Graduate-level courses in accounting, economics, finance, and operations management.

United States Dept. of Agriculture Graduate School
Director, Correspondence School
STOP 9911, Room 1112
1400 Independence Avenue, SW
Washington, DC 20250-9911
Phone: (202) 720-7123
Fax: (202) 690-1516
E-mail: correspond@grad.usda.gov
Web site: grad.usda.gov/cores/corpro.html

One graduate-level course in statistics and sample survey methods.

Université de Moncton
Education Permanente
Moncton, NB E1A 3E9
Canada
Phone: (506) 858-4121
Fax: (506) 858-4489
E-mail: blancha@umoncton.ca
Web site: www.umoncton.ca/educ-perm/eduperm.html

Graduate-level courses in accounting, finance, management, and marketing.

University of Baltimore
Merrick School of Business
1420 North Charles Street
Baltimore, MD 21201
Phone: (410) 837-4987
Fax: (410) 837-5652
E-mail: dgerlowski@ubmail.ubalt.edu

Graduate-level courses in economics and management.

University of Colorado at Boulder
Program Manager
Division of Continuing Education
Boulder, CO 80309-3962
Phone: (303) 492-8756 • (800) 331-2801
Fax: (303) 492-3962
E-mail: cewww@colorado.edu
Web site: www.colorado.edu/cewww

Graduate-level courses in business.

University of Colorado at Colorado Springs
Graduate School of Business Administration
1420 Austin Bluffs Parkway
P.O. Box 7150
Colorado Springs, CO 80933
Phone: (719) 262-3401
Fax: (719) 262-3494
E-mail: bneiberg@mail.uccs.edu
Web site: www.uccs.edu/~collbus

Graduate-level courses in accounting, finance, international business, management, management information systems, marketing, operations management, and production management.

University of Colorado at Denver
Graduate College of Business
Campus Box 165
P.O. Box 173364
Denver, CO 80217
Phone: (303) 556-6517
Fax: (303) 556-5904
E-mail: teri_burleson@maroon.cudenver.edu
Web site: www.cudenver.edu

Graduate-level courses in accounting, business information science, and financial management/planning.

University of Missouri-Kansas City
Henry W. Bloch School of Business and
    Public Administration
5100 Rockhill Road
Kansas City, MO 64110
Phone: (816) 235-1012
Fax: (816) 235-2206
E-mail: wbeddy@cctr.umkc.edu
Web site: www.umkc.edu

Graduate-level courses in accounting, finance, human resources, international business, management information systems, manufacturing management, marketing, and strategic management.

University of New Orleans
College of Business
Room BA-273
Business Building
New Orleans, LA 70148-1520
Phone: (504) 280-6393
Fax: (504) 280-6958
E-mail: pjhmk@uno.edu
Web site: www.uno.edu

Graduate-level courses in finance and marketing.

University of New South Wales
Australian Graduate School of Management
Sydney, NSW 2052
Australia
Phone: (02) 99319206
Fax: (02) 99319206
E-mail: carolynp@agsm.unsw.edu.au
Web site: www.agsm.unsw.edu.au

Graduate-level courses in accounting, finance, human resources, information management, management, marketing, and strategic management.

University of Phoenix
University of Phoenix Online Campus—Center
  for Distance Education
4615 East Elwood
Phoenix, AZ 85040
Phone: (480) 921-8014
Fax: (480) 894-2152
Web site: www.uophx.edu

Graduate-level courses in accounting, business communications, business ethics, business information science, business law, business policy/strategy, economics, finance, human resources, information management, international business, international management, management, marketing, and public relations.

University of Sarasota
College of Business Administration
5250 17th Street
Sarasota, FL 34235
Phone: (941) 379-0404
Fax: (941) 379-9464
E-mail: 71722.2373@compuserve.com
Web site: www.sarasota-
  online.com/university/graduate

Graduate-level courses in finance, human resources, international business, international trade, management, management information systems, and marketing.

University of St. Francis
College of Graduate Studies
500 Wilcox Street
Joliet, IL 60435
Phone: (800) 735-4723
Fax: (815) 740-3537
E-mail: jthompson@stfrancis.edu
Web site: www.stfrancis.edu

Graduate-level courses in management, marketing, and research and development administration.

Appendix D: For More Information on Schools in This Book

If you have questions about one of the schools described in this book, don't hesitate to write to us. We'll do our best to help. These are the ground rules:

What to do before writing to us

Point your web browser to www.degree.net/updates/mba. At this web site we will post updates and corrections to the school listings in this book.

Do your own homework. Check with your local library, the relevant state education department, or the Better Business Bureau first, as well as, of course, searching for them on the Internet. Any major search engine should locate a school's Web site. There is, for instance, a complete university list in the "universities" section of www.yahoo.com.

Schools do move, and the post office will only forward mail for a short while. If a letter comes back as "undeliverable," call directory assistance ("information") in the school's city and see if a number is listed. They can give you a new street address as well.

Schools do change phone numbers, and the telephone company will only notify you of the new number for a short while. If you can't reach a school by phone, write to it, or try information to see if there has been a change.

Writing to us

If you cannot reach a school by phone or mail, if you have new information you think we should know, or if you have questions or problems, then please write and let us know. We may be able to help.

Enclose a self-addressed, stamped envelope. If you are outside the United States, enclose two international postal reply coupons, available at your post office.

If you want extensive advice or opinions on your personal situation, you will need to use the Degree Consulting Service that John established (although he no longer runs it). This service is described in Appendix F.

Don't get too annoyed if we don't respond promptly. We do our best, but we get overwhelmed sometimes, and we travel a lot.

Please don't telephone.

Write to both authors at the following address:

John & Mariah Bear
Degree.net
C/O Ten Speed Press
PO Box 7123
Berkeley, CA 94707 USA

Or email:
john.bear@degree.net
mariah.bear@degree.net

Do let us know of any mistakes or outdated information you find in this book; we will post corrections at www.degree.net/updates/mba.

Appendix E: For Information on Schools Not in This Book

There are three reasons why a school in which you might be interested is not described in this book:

1. **It might be relevant, but we chose not to designate it one of the best schools.**

2. **It is not relevant for this book since it does not offer degrees entirely or mostly by home study.**

3. **It does not have recognized accreditation.**

If you have questions about a school that is not described in this book, here is what we suggest, in the following order:

1. Check *Bears' Guide to Earning Degrees by Distance Learning*, which is a complete source for all distance-learning programs, and is published by Ten Speed Press. In it we list over 2000 schools that offer degrees by home study—good, bad, and otherwise. For more information, write to Degree.net c/o Ten Speed Press, PO Box 7123, Berkeley CA 94707, or visit our web site at www.degree.net.

2. Look it up in one of the standard school directories that you can find in any public library or bookstore: Lovejoy's, Barron's, Peterson's, Patterson's, ARCO, and half a dozen others. These books describe virtually every traditional college and university in the United States and Canada.

3. Ask for the help of a reference librarian. Your tax dollars pay their salaries.

4. If you know the location of the school, even just the state, check with the relevant state education agency.

If none of the above approaches produce any useful information, then write to us and we will do what we can to help.

Enclose a self-addressed, stamped envelope.

If you want extensive advice or opinions on your personal situation, you will need to use the Degree Consulting Service described in Appendix D. Don't get too annoyed if we don't respond promptly. We do our best, but we both get overwhelmed sometimes, and we travel a lot.

Please don't telephone.

Write to both authors at the following address:

John & Mariah Bear
Degree.net
C/O Ten Speed Press
PO Box 7123
Berkeley, CA 94707

john.bear@degree.net
mariah.bear@degree.net

Appendix F: For Personal Advice on Your Own Situation

If you would like advice and recommendations on your own specific situation, a personal counseling service offers this information, by mail only. John started this service in 1977 at the request of many readers. While he still remains a consultant, since 1981 the actual consulting and personal evaluations have been done by two of his colleagues (and friends), who are leading experts in the field of nontraditional education.

For a modest consulting fee, these things are done:

1. You will get a long personal letter evaluating your situation, recommending the best degree programs for you (including part-time programs in your area, if relevant) and estimating how long it will take and what it will cost you to complete your degree(s).

2. You will get answers to any specific questions you may have with regard to programs you may now be considering, institutions you have already dealt with, or other relevant matters.

3. You will get detailed, up-to-the-minute information on institutions and degree programs, equivalency exams, sources of the correspondence courses you may need, career opportunities, resume writing, sources of financial aid, and other topics in the form of extensive prepared notes.

4. You will be entitled to telephone the service for a full year for unlimited follow-up counseling, to keep updated on new programs and other changes, and to otherwise use the service as your personal information resource.

If you are interested in this personal counseling, please write or call and you will be sent descriptive literature and a counseling questionnaire, without cost or obligation.

If, once you have these materials, you do want counseling, simply fill out the questionnaire and return it, with a letter and resume if you like, along with the fee. Your personal reply and counseling materials will be airmailed to you as quickly as possible.

For free information, write or telephone:

Degree Consulting Services
P.O. Box 3533
Santa Rosa, CA 95402
Phone: (707) 539-6466
Fax: (707) 538-3577
E-mail: degrees@sonic.net.

Web site: www.sonic.net/~degrees

Note: Use this address only to reach the counseling service. For all other matters, please write to:

John & Mariah Bear

Degree.net
C/O Ten Speed Press
PO Box 7123
Berkeley, CA 94707

Appendix G: Bending the Rules

One of the most common complaints or admonishments we hear from readers goes something like this: "You said thus-and-so, but when I inquired of the school, they told me such-and-such." It has happened (although rarely) that a school claims that a program we have written about does not exist. Sometimes a student achieves something (such as completing a certain degree entirely by correspondence) that we had been told by a high official of the school was impossible.

One of the open secrets in the world of higher education is that the rules are constantly being bent. But as with the Emperor's new clothes, no one dares to point and say what is really going on, especially in print.

Unfortunately, we cannot provide many specific examples of bent rules, naming names and all. This is for two good reasons:

1. Many situations where students profit from bent rules would disappear in an instant if anyone dared mention the situation publicly. There is, for instance, a major state university that is forbidden by its charter from granting degrees for correspondence study. But they regularly work out special arrangements for students who are carried on the books as residential students even though all work is done by mail. Indeed, some graduates have never set foot on campus. If this ever got out, the Board of Trustees, the relevant accrediting agency, and all the other universities in that state would probably have conniptions, and the practice would be suspended at once.

2. These kinds of things can change so rapidly, particularly with new personnel or new policies, that a listing of anomalies and curious practices would probably be obsolete before the ink dried.

Consider a few examples of the sort of thing that is going on in higher education every day, whether or not anyone will admit it, except perhaps behind closed doors or after several drinks:

A friend of John's at a major university was unable to complete one required course for her Doctorate before she had to leave for another state. This university does not offer correspondence courses, but she was able to convince a professor to enroll her in a regular course, which she would just happen never to visit in person.

A man in graduate school needed to be enrolled in nine units of coursework each semester to keep his employer's tuition-assistance plan going. But his job was too demanding one year, and he was unable to do so. The school enrolled him in nine units of "independent study" for which no work was asked or required, and for which a "pass" grade was given.

A woman at a large school needed to get a certain number of units before an inflexible time deadline. When it was clear she was not going to make it, a kindly professor turned in grades for her, and told her she could do the actual coursework later on.

A major state university offers nonresident degrees for people living in that state only. When a reader wrote to John saying that he, living a thousand miles from that state, was able to complete his degree entirely by correspondence, we asked a contact at that school what was going on. "We will take students from anywhere in our correspondence degree program," she told us. "But for God's sake, don't print that in your book, or we'll be deluged with applicants."

Please use this information prudently. It will probably do no good to pound on a table and say, "What do you mean, I can't do this? John Bear says that rules don't mean anything, anyway." But when faced with a problem, it surely can do no harm to remember that there do exist many situations in which the rules have turned out to be far less rigid than the printed literature of a school would lead you to believe.

Index of Concentrations and Specializations

Accounting
Central Queensland University
Deakin University
Florida Gulf Coast University
Keller Graduate School of Management
Northeastern Illinois University
University of Phoenix Online
University of Southern Queensland

Administration
Central Michigan University

Agriculture
Athabasca University
Purdue University
University of Guelph

Banking
Florida Gulf Coast University
Morehead State University

Business Communication
Jones International University

Communications Technology
Capella University

Construction & Real Estate
College of Estate Management
University of Paisley

Design Management
University of Westminster

E-commerce
Deakin University
Jones International University
Touro University International

Economics
Deakin University

Education
Deakin University
Oxford Brookes University
University of Leicester

Entrepreneurship & Small Business
Florida Gulf Coast University
Jones International University
Southern Cross University
Stephens College

Environmental Management
University of Southern Queensland

Estate & Personal Finance Planning
City University
College of Financial Planning

Finance
American College
Auburn University

Bellevue University
Central Queensland University
City University
College for Financial Planning
Dalhousie University
Deakin University
Florida Gulf Coast University
Institute for Financial Management
Keller Graduate School of Management
Northeastern Illinois University
Southern Cross University
University of Leicester
University of San Francisco
University of Sarasota
University of Southern Queensland
University of Wisconsin—Whitewater

General Business
Athabasca University
Ball State
California State University,
    Dominguez Hills
Capella University
Charles Sturt
City University
Colorado State University
Deakin University
Drexel University
Edith Cowan University
Empire State College
Georgia Southern University
Henley Management College
Heriot-Watt University
Hong Kong Baptist University
Indiana University
Kettering University
Lehigh University
Liberty University
Marylhurst University
National University
New York Institute of Technology
Nova Southeastern University
Ohio University
Oklahoma State University
Old Dominion University
Open University of Hong Kong
Open University
Oxford Brookes University
Pace University
Portland State University
Purdue University
Ramkhamhaeng University
Regent University
Regis University
Rensselaer Polytechnic Institute
Saint Leo University
Salve Regina University

Strayer University
Texas A&M University
Touro University International
Université de Moncton
University of Colorado—Colorado
 Springs
University of Durham
University of Florida
University of Leicester
University of Maryland
University of Natal
University of Northumbria at
 Newcastle
University of Notre Dame
University of Phoenix
University of Phoenix Online
University of Pittsburgh
University of Strathclyde
University of Surrey
University of Warwick
University of Western Ontario

Healthcare Administration
Auburn University
Florida Gulf Coast University
Jones International University
Keller Graduate School
Morehead State University
Saint Joseph's College
Southern Cross University
Touro University International
University of Dallas
University of Phoenix
University of Saint Francis
University of Saint Thomas
University of Sarasota

Human Resources
Auburn University
Central Queensland University
Deakin University
Florida Gulf Coast University
Keller Graduate School
Morehead State University
Salve Regina University
Southern Cross University
University of Leicester
University of Sarasota
University of Southern Queensland

Information Systems & Technology
Athabasca University
Auburn University
Central Queensland University
City University
Colorado State University
Florida Gulf Coast University
ISIM University
Jones International University
Keller Graduate School
Morehead State University
Southwest Missouri State University
Stephens College

Touro University International
University of Southern Queensland
Worcester Polytechnic Institute

International Business
Bellevue University
Central Queensland University
Colorado State University
Deakin University
Duke University
Jones International University
Keller Graduate School
Madonna University
Napier University
Open University of the Netherlands
 (European Business)
Salve Regina University
Southern Cross University
Touro University International
University of London
University of Maryland
University of Phoenix
University of Phoenix Online
University of San Francisco
University of Sarasota
University of Southern Queensland
University of Texas at Dallas

Law
Deakin University
Nottingham Trent University Law
 School
University of Southern Queensland

Leadership
Bellevue University
City University
Deakin University

Management
Capella University
Central Michigan University
Central Queensland University
Clarkson College
Duke University
Florida Gulf Coast University
Keller Graduate School
Lesley College
Purdue University
Regent University
Salve Regina University
Southern Cross University
Stephens College
Syracuse University
Thomas Edison State College
University of London
University of Maryland
University of Saint Francis
University of San Francisco
University of Wisconsin—
 Whitewater

Manufacturing
Florida Gulf Coast University

Marketing
Auburn University
Central Queensland University
City University
Deakin University
Florida Gulf Coast University
Keller Graduate School
Southern Cross University
University of Leicester
University of Paisley
University of San Francisco
University of Sarasota
University of Southern Queensland
University of Wisconsin—
 Whitewater
Worcester Polytechnic Institute

Occupational Health and Safety
University of Southern Queensland

Operations Management
Auburn University
Florida Gulf Coast University
Madonna University
Worcester Polytechnic Institute

Project Management
Henley Management College
Jones International University
Keller Graduate School
University of Southern Queensland

Public Sector Management
Central Queensland University
Deakin University

Quality
Madonna University
University of Paisley

Retailing & Wholesaling
University of Stirling

Sports Management
Southern Cross University

Technology Management
Auburn University
University of Phoenix
University of Phoenix Online
Worcester Polytechnic Institute

Telecommunications Management
Keller Graduate School
Oklahoma State University
University of San Francisco

Tourism
Bournemouth University
Central Queensland University
Southern Cross University